Level D

Word Wisdom

Vocabulary for Listening, Speaking, Reading, and Writing

Author
Jerry Zutell, Ph.D.
The Ohio State University

D1501095

Credits: Located on last page of book

ISBN: 0-7367-2448-6

Copyright © 2005 Zaner-Bloser, Inc.

Zaner-Bloser, Inc., P.O. Box 16764, Columbus, Ohio 43216-6764 (1-800-421-3018)
www.zaner-bloser.com

A ZB Language Arts Program

Contents

4 UNIT THEME: Behavior   72

5 UNIT THEME Movement   94

6 UNIT THEME Appearance　116

7 UNIT THEME Relationships　138

8 UNIT THEME Good and Bad　160

Context Clues

for Word Wisdom

The Apparition

Perhaps you've heard that "seeing is believing." Sometimes, however, what we think we see can be misleading.

Dr. Fogg sat down for lunch with his oldest friend, Professor Linear. "What new research have you been working on?" Professor Linear asked.

Dr. Fogg answered, "It's very exciting. I have produced an **apparition** in my lab on many occasions."

"An apparition! How did you create a ghostly image in a laboratory? Please **enlighten** me," the professor begged. "Do you have **evidence** to support your claim?"

"Of course," answered the doctor, polishing his thick glasses with the napkin on his lap. "I **expect** to show the world my supporting facts soon. I hope to **televise** my results next month."

"Fogg, I would love a **preview** of your lab work before you go on television."

The two men met the next day in Dr. Fogg's office. "Bad news," Fogg reported. "The lamp has burned out, and I cannot see the apparition."

Professor Linear offered to replace the light bulb. "Ah, there it is! The light made a **noticeable** difference," exclaimed Dr. Fogg.

"I see nothing," responded Professor Linear. "May I see your research notes?"

"I'm afraid my notes are not **legible,**" said Dr. Fogg, taking off his eyeglasses to clean them on his lab coat. "Even I can barely read my own writing. Hmm, the apparition seems to **vanish** when I take off my glasses."

"May I look?" asked the professor, picking up the glasses. "Dear Fogg, you have polished these glasses so much that they are terribly scratched. The apparition you claim to have seen is simply a reflection on the scratched lens!"

"Imagine, Professor, if I had gone on TV to share my evidence! It's a good thing we had the **foresight** to bring you here!"

"A better thing," said Fogg's friend, "would be for you to get new glasses."

Sight

UNIT

1

Context Clues Strategy

Look for Words That Mean the Same

EXAMPLE: Tim's *vision* is not as good as it once was. His eyesight is so weak that he has to wear glasses.

CLUE: The word *eyesight* is a definition for the word *vision* and helps explain its meaning.

Here are steps for using this context clues strategy to figure out the meaning of the word *apparition*.

Read the sentence with the unknown word and some of the sentences around it.

• • • • •

*"I have produced an **apparition** in my lab on many occasions."*
"An apparition! How did you create a ghostly image in a laboratory?"

Look for context clues. Can you find **Words That Mean the Same** as the word *apparition*?

• • • • •

When Professor Linear hears Dr. Fogg tell about an *apparition*, he asks how Fogg created a *ghostly image*.

Think about the context clues and other information you may already know.

• • • • •

Ghostly image tells the meaning of *apparition*.

Predict a meaning for the word.

• • • • •

An *apparition* is probably a ghostly image.

Check the Word Wisdom Dictionary to be sure of the meaning.

• • • • •

The word *apparition* means "a ghostly-looking image."

Practice the Strategy Here is another boldfaced word from the story about Dr. Fogg on page 6. Using the context clues strategy on page 7, follow these steps to figure out the meaning of the word.

evidence

Read the sentence that includes the word *evidence*. Read some of the sentences around the word.

Look for context clues. What **Words That Mean the Same** can you find?

_____

_____

_____

Think about the context clues. What other helpful information do you know?

_____

_____

_____

Predict a meaning for the word *evidence*.

_____

_____

Check the Word Wisdom Dictionary to be sure of the meaning of the word *evidence*. Decide which of the meanings fits the context.

_____

_____

_____

WORD LIST

✔ apparition
enlighten
✔ evidence
expect
televise
preview
noticeable
legible
vanish
foresight

Use Context Clues You have been introduced to two vocabulary words from "The Apparition." Those words are checked off in the Word List here. Under "Vocabulary Word" below, write the other eight words from the Word List. Predict a meaning for each word under "Your Prediction." Then check the meanings in the Word Wisdom Dictionary. Write the definition under "Dictionary Says."

	Vocabulary Word	Your Prediction	Dictionary Says
1			
2			
3			
4			
5			
6			
7			
8			

Process the Meanings

Find the Synonyms Choose a word from the Word List that means the SAME or NEARLY THE SAME as each word below. Write the synonym on the line next to the word.

1 disappear _____

3 readable _____

2 facts _____

4 ghost _____

Rewrite the Sentences Rewrite each sentence. Use the word in parentheses. You may add an ending to the word.

5 I watched a sample of several new movies. (preview)

_____

_____

6 It's helpful to plan ahead when you go camping. (foresight)

_____

_____

7 The games will be shown on television. (televise)

_____

_____

8 Would you please explain that to me? (enlighten)

_____

_____

9 Mud is easily seen on a clean floor. (noticeable)

_____

10 What time do you look forward to doing your homework? (expect)

_____

Apply What You've Learned

Solve Riddles Solve each riddle with a word from the Word List.

1 You can't see this, but it's useful for planning. _____

2 If you said you saw one of these, your friends might think you were seeing things. _____

3 Without this, you can't solve a mystery. _____

4 If you had a messy room and you wanted to go out to play, you might wish the mess would do this. _____

Connect to Your Life Respond to each question or statement.

5 Why is a **preview** of a book useful?

_____

6 Describe a time when someone **enlightened** you about something.

_____

7 What might happen if you write a message that is not **legible**?

_____

8 Describe what was **noticeable** when you arrived at school today.

_____

9 Describe something that you **expect** to happen tomorrow.

_____

10 Describe something **televised** that you found surprising.

_____

 Write It! Imagine that your favorite book, CD, or video game has disappeared from your room. How would you solve the mystery? Use several words from the Word List on page 10.

PART 2 Latin Roots

for Word Wisdom

More Than Double Vision:
Flies' Eyes

Do you understand how we see? First, light travels through space from the sun, a lamp, or another light source. This light strikes objects in its path. The objects absorb some of the light and reflect the rest. When you look at something, you see the reflected light.

Not all living things see in the same way that humans do. Did you ever **inspect** the eyes of a fly or of another insect? Insects and certain other living things have compound eyes. We have single eyes. If you can, find a dead fly and study this **specimen**. You will find that a compound eye has a strange **appearance**. Make sure you wash your hands when you are finished!

A compound eye is made of hundreds or even thousands of units. Each unit is like our single eye in some ways. The unit has its own **transparent,** or clear, lens and a nerve that leads to the insect's brain.

The units in compound eyes are different from our eyes, too. Each unit faces in a slightly different direction. It sees only a small, **specific** part of the insect's surroundings. The insect's brain blends the **visual** images from all of these units into one image.

Our eyes can change focus. They allow us to see close up or far away. A compound eye cannot change focus. That gives insects a limited **perspective**. They see only what is close by. Still, compound eyes **provide** insects with a vital skill. This kind of eye is very good at detecting motion. And because the eye bulges out, it can see up, down, forward, backward, and to the sides—all at the same time. This skill is **apparent** to anyone who has ever tried to swat a fly!

Compound eyes allow insects to fly at high speeds without running into anything. Insects see changes in their surroundings quickly, allowing them to swerve to miss an object in their path. This skill also helps them chase—and catch— other flying insects.

So flies and other insects don't need a **visa** or a passport to go sightseeing around the world— they can see only a few feet away! All they really need is something to eat and people to annoy!

Practice the Context Clues Strategy Here is one of the boldfaced words from the selection on page 12. Use the context clues strategy you learned in Part 1 on page 7 to figure out the meaning of the word.

transparent

Read the sentence that uses the word *transparent*. Read some of the sentences around the word.

Look for context clues to the word's meaning. What **Words That Mean the Same** can you find?

_____

_____

_____

Think about the context clues. What other helpful information do you know?

_____

_____

Predict a meaning for the word *transparent*.

_____

_____

_____

Check your Word Wisdom Dictionary to be sure of the meaning of the word *transparent*. Which of the meanings for the word *transparent* fits the context?

_____

_____

_____

Unlock the Meanings

Many English words are made from Latin roots. If you know the meanings of different roots, you can unlock the meanings of many new words. Several words you learned in Part 1 have a Latin root. Each root is related to seeing.

Latin Root: **par**
meaning: to appear
English word: *apparition*
meaning: a ghostly-looking image

Latin Root: **spec, spect, spic**
meaning: to see, to look
English word: *to expect*
meaning: to look forward to

Latin Root: **vid, vis**
meaning: to see
English word: *evidence*
meaning: facts leading to proof

WORD LIST

inspect
specimen
appearance
transparent
specific
visual
perspective
provide
apparent
visa

Sort by Roots Find these roots in the Word List. Write each word on a line under the correct root. Then think of other words you know that come from the same Latin roots. Write each word in the correct place.

Sight

Latin Root:
par

Latin Root:
spec, spect, spic

Latin Root:
vid, vis

Prefix	Meaning
trans-	across, through
in-	in, into
pro-	forward, for

Example

trans- (through) + par (appear) + -ent
= **transparent**

Use Roots and Prefixes Circle any root or prefix you find in the boldfaced words below. Use context clues, roots, and prefixes to write the meaning of each word. Check your definitions in the Word Wisdom Dictionary.

1 The guard **inspected** the contents of our bags. _____

2 We recognized Alice's face because her **appearance** hadn't changed.

_____

3 Please **provide** your phone number so that I can call you.

_____

4 The butterfly is a **specimen** of the monarch variety.

_____

5 Talking to many people gives me a new **perspective** on solving the

problem. _____

6 It was **apparent** that we arrived for dinner on the wrong day, because

no one was home. _____

7 A stop sign is a **visual** signal. _____

8 Windows are **transparent**, but you cannot see through walls.

_____

9 Do you have any **specific** plans for vacation, such as where you will

go and when? _____

10 Students from other countries need a government **visa** to study in the

United States. _____

_____

Process the Meanings

WORD LIST

- inspect
- specimen
- appearance
- transparent
- specific
- visual
- perspective
- provide
- apparent
- visa

Choose the Words Read the pair of related boldfaced words in the sentence. Circle the word that completes each sentence correctly.

1 The scientist found a **specific**, **specimen** of a frog with yellow spots.

2 It is **apparent**, **transparent** that you did not study for the test.

3 My parents **provide**, **visa** the things I need for school.

4 Glass is **apparent**, **transparent**, but paper is not.

5 The dentist will **perspective**, **inspect** your teeth.

6 Please give me **specific**, **specimen** directions so that I can find your house.

Find the Words Write the word from the Word List that best completes each sentence.

7 The star put in an _____ at the opening of her latest movie.

8 Before traveling overseas, you may have to get a tourist's _____.

9 What does a person look like from a dog's _____?

10 The doormat is a _____ reminder to wipe your feet.

Apply What You've Learned

Demonstrate Word Knowledge Answer the questions or follow the directions.

1 Would you like to live in a house with **transparent** walls? Explain.

_____

2 Name two kinds of people who might **inspect** things.

_____

3 What is your **perspective** on learning another language?

_____

4 Describe what you like best about your **appearance**.

_____

5 Describe an object in the room. Give three **visual** clues.

_____

6 Is it always **apparent** if a dog is friendly or unfriendly? Explain.

_____

7 What kinds of **specimens** might a scientist collect?

_____

8 If you had to **provide** a snack for the class, what would you do?

_____

9 When does a person need a **visa**? _____

_____

10 Give three **specific** details about the clothes you are wearing.

_____

Speak It! Describe a movie or play you have seen. Use several words from the Word List on page 16.

Reference Skills

for Word Wisdom

Come and See "My House"!

Trash is everywhere! It's around your home, streets, and school. Even if you pick up the trash, what should you do with it? Will it end up in a landfill? Can it be recycled?

When you **scan** all of your surroundings, do you see too much trash? Can you **distinguish** between a plastic bottle that can be recycled and one that can't? You can brush up on recycling at "My House," an **exhibit** at the Columbus Zoo and Aquarium in Columbus, Ohio. It **resembles** a regular house—until you walk inside.

There are three habitats that make up the living room of "My House." They are a marsh, a forest, and a prairie. As you walk through, you learn how these habitats are **distinct** from each other. In the marsh, you can climb on lily pads and search for frog eggs and fish. In the forest, you can get tangled in a giant spiderweb or explore a hollowed-out tree. You can also **observe** the insects, reptiles, and tall grasses that live in the prairie.

The bedroom of the house **demonstrates** how these habitats are threatened. You learn how harmful trash is, and you see how exhaust from cars and smoke from factories pollute the air. You also hear how building roads and houses can destroy natural habitats.

In the kitchen of "My House," you learn ways to conserve Earth's resources. Some of the ways are **obvious,** such as not wasting electricity or water. Other ways might be new to you, like using cleaning products that will not harm the environment. Visitors are asked to look for the recycling **emblem,** or symbol, before they buy a product. They are also shown how to **detect** water leaks so that water is not wasted. Visitors are shown how recycled products can be used again. In fact, the whole house was built from recycled products. The outside walls are a mixture of cement and disposable lunch trays that were collected from 63 local schools. The floors were made from recycled tires. The house's roof, siding, and chairs were also made from recycled products.

If your community has an exhibit like this one, be sure to go see it. You can help make your environment safer and healthier. At the same time, you can protect natural habitats!

Practice the Context Clues Strategy Here is one of the boldfaced words from the selection on page 18. Use the context clues strategy you learned in Part 1 on page 7 to figure out the meaning of the word.

emblem

📖 **Read** the sentence that uses the word *emblem* and some of the sentences around it.

🔍 **Look** for context clues to the word's meaning. What **Words That Mean the Same** can you find?

_____

_____

_____

💡 **Think** about the context clues. What other helpful information do you know?

_____

_____

➡️ **Predict** a meaning for the word *emblem*.

_____

_____

_____

✔️ **Check** your Word Wisdom Dictionary to be sure of the meaning of the word *emblem*. Write the definition here.

_____

_____

_____

Idioms and Special Dictionaries An **idiom** is a phrase or an expression that has a special meaning. You can't understand an idiom from the meaning of each separate word. You can look up unfamiliar idioms in a dictionary of idioms like *A Dictionary of American Idioms* to learn their meanings. Read this sentence:

> We *never pass notes in class because our teacher has eyes in the back of her head.*

The words *has eyes in the back of her head* form an idiom. The phrase means "can see things without seeming to look."

Match the Meanings Read the sentences below. Each underlined idiom relates to one of the words in the Word List on page 21. Look up the meaning of the idiom in a dictionary of idioms. Match the idiom with the vocabulary word it relates to. Write the word on the line.

1 The answer was <u>as plain as the nose on my face.</u>

_____

2 The twins were <u>like two peas in a pod.</u>

_____

3 The dishonest man will <u>show his true colors</u> by taking a bribe.

_____

4 Those two are <u>as different as night and day.</u>

_____

5 <u>Keep your eyes peeled</u> during the magic trick to see how easy it is.

_____

Find the Meaning
1. Use context clues.
2. Look for a familiar root, prefix, or suffix.
3. If the context or a word part doesn't help, check the dictionary.

Define the Words Follow the steps above to write the meaning of each boldfaced word. Then write 1, 2, or 3 to show which steps you used.

1 Most people can **distinguish** a dog from a cat.

_____

2 When I sing in the choir, I **scan** the audience for my family.

_____

3 Ohio has four seasons with **distinct** weather.

_____

4 Do you **resemble** your mother?

_____

5 Please **observe** how to make a bed so that you can do it.

_____

6 You sound very serious, but I **detect** a smile on your face.

_____

7 It's **obvious** by your high score that you studied for the test.

_____

8 The eagle is an **emblem** that appears on U.S. money.

_____

9 The artist's **exhibit** was worth seeing!

_____

10 Our teacher will **demonstrate** how to use the microscope.

_____

WORD LIST

scan
distinguish
exhibit
resemble
distinct
observe
demonstrate
obvious
emblem
detect

WORD LIST

scan
distinguish
exhibit
resemble
distinct
observe
demonstrate
obvious
emblem
detect

Choose the Correct Word Write the word from the Word List that best completes each sentence. You may need to add or change an ending for some words.

1 Our team chose the tiger as the _____ for our uniforms.

2 The paintings at the art _____ are all for sale.

3 Can you _____ between a cockatoo and a cocker spaniel?

4 With careful examination, I could _____ signs of a struggle around the fishbowl.

5 Please _____ for me how to set the table properly.

6 It is _____ that Jill has grown. Her shoes are two sizes bigger now.

7 My mother and I _____ each other.

8 Paul _____ the want ads each day to look for a job.

9 Many historic homes have _____ architecture, so each one is unique.

10 Please _____ how well the puppy behaves when I give a command.

Apply What You've Learned

Answer the Questions Answer each question below.

1 What **emblem** would you like to use for a team or club? Why?

_____

2 In what ways can you be **distinguished** from your friends?

_____

3 What skill would you be proud to **demonstrate** for an audience?

_____

4 How do you **detect** feelings of happiness in a friend?

_____

5 How can you make an **exhibit** out of your favorite photos?

_____

6 Which family member do you most **resemble**?

_____

Build a Word Ladder Use the words in the box to complete each word ladder below. Order each list from most (top) to least (bottom). Use a dictionary if needed.

> glance   obvious   scan   hidden

7 _____   MOST   observe _____

distinct   ↓
          to   **9** _____

8 _____   ↓
          LEAST   **10** _____

Write It! Write a paragraph to compare and contrast two things or two people. Use as many words from the Word List on page 22 as you can.

Review

for Word Wisdom

Sort by Parts of Speech Sort the words in the Word List by their part of speech. Write each word in the correct column. If a word can be more than one part of speech, write it in every column that applies.

WORD LIST

- apparition
- enlighten
- evidence
- expect
- televise
- preview
- noticeable
- legible
- vanish
- foresight
- inspect
- specimen
- appearance
- transparent
- specific
- visual
- perspective
- provide
- apparent
- visa
- scan
- distinguish
- exhibit
- resemble
- distinct
- observe
- demonstrate
- obvious
- emblem
- detect

Nouns (words that name a person, place, or thing)	Verbs (action words)	Adjectives (words that describe)

Use Multiple Meanings Some words in this unit have more than one meaning. Look up the words *scan* and *preview* in your Word Wisdom Dictionary. Write two sentences for each word. Show that you understand two different meanings for each word.

scan

1 _____

2 _____

preview

3 _____

4 _____

Use Related Words Answer the questions. Use the word in parentheses in your response.

5 What similar qualities do tropical birds **exhibit**? (resemble)

_____

6 How can you **distinguish** between a kindergartner and a fourth grader? (observe)

_____

7 What would you do if you saw an **apparition**? (appearance)

_____

8 If someone **inspected** your desk, what would he or she think? (expect)

_____

9 Does seeing a **preview** of a TV show make you want to watch it? (televise)

_____

10 Can you **detect** when someone has been in your room? (evidence)

_____

Taking Vocabulary Tests

TEST-TAKING STRATEGY

Some vocabulary tests ask you to choose the meaning of a word in a phrase or sentence. Every answer choice will fit the sentence, so context will not help you decide on an answer. You can narrow your choices by first throwing out the answers you know are wrong.

Sample:

a <u>brilliant</u> star
○ dull
◉ bright
○ large
○ new

Practice Test Read each phrase. Fill in the circle for the word or words that have the SAME or NEARLY THE SAME meaning as the underlined word.

1 her <u>legible</u> handwriting
○ unusual
○ easy-to-read
○ confusing
○ beautiful

2 to mysteriously <u>vanish</u>
○ appear
○ escape
○ grow larger
○ disappear

3 an <u>enlightening</u> class
○ informative
○ long
○ boring
○ difficult

4 a unique <u>perspective</u>
○ look
○ subject
○ behavior
○ point of view

5 a <u>visual</u> clue
○ unimportant
○ small
○ visible
○ strange

6 a <u>transparent</u> material
○ heavy
○ clear
○ hidden
○ colorful

7 <u>specific</u> instructions
○ detailed
○ short
○ wordy
○ foreign

8 a familiar <u>emblem</u>
○ sight
○ saying
○ symbol
○ sound

9 an important <u>specimen</u>
○ group of men
○ meeting
○ speech
○ sample

10 to <u>provide</u> an answer
○ pay no attention to
○ give
○ ask for
○ argue with

Build New Words

Use Suffixes The suffix *-ly* can make a word into an adverb. Adverbs tell **how** or **to what extent**. Words ending in a vowel may drop the vowel before adding *-ly*. Use the suffix *-ly* to form new words. Then use each new word in a sentence.

Word	+ Suffix	= New Word	Sentence
distinct	-ly		
obvious	-ly		
apparent	-ly		
legible	-ly		
noticeable	-ly		

Speak It! Keep your eyes open for the words in this unit. Tell about an amazing sight you would like to see sometime.

Context Clues

for Word Wisdom

Yesterday and Today:
The Yucatán Peninsula

For as long as people have lived, they have wondered about the earth. Today scientists are learning even more about the earth through new exploration. Read this article about underground rivers and caves in Mexico.

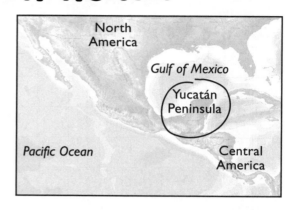

North America

Gulf of Mexico

Yucatán Peninsula

Pacific Ocean

Central America

Beneath the jungles of Mexico lie underground caves and rivers. The story of how they got there began when dinosaurs roamed the earth.

A **meteorite** fell from space and hit the earth sixty-five million years ago. It struck the part of Mexico that is known today as the Yucatán **peninsula**. The Yucatán is an arm of land that sticks out into the Gulf of Mexico and the Caribbean Sea. The meteorite that hit the Yucatán was huge. It left a bowl-shaped dent, or **crater,** one hundred and ten miles across.

The **disaster** had lasting effects. Many scientists believe that dust rose into the air and blocked the light and heat from the sun. Without the sun, the dinosaurs all died. The land also changed. The **limestone,** the soft rock that forms the jungle floor, began to develop cracks. Those cracks filled with rainwater. In some places, the cracks grew larger. The water kept wearing away the rock. This eventually created **caverns** deep in the earth. These large hollow caves often join **sinkholes**. The sinkholes are areas that have sunk below the land around them. Some sinkholes have a small opening at the top to the land above. Some have a wider opening, and others have no opening at all.

There are no above-ground rivers in the Yucatán. But underground rivers flow through the caverns. Rainwater and the underground rivers provide the region's only fresh water.

Archaeologists are exploring these rivers and **aquatic** caverns. In some of the underground caverns, they have found skulls, bones, and other **fossils** of humans and animals. These objects, or remains, teach us about the history of the earth.

Context Clues Strategy

Look for the Location or Setting

EXAMPLE: The diver put on his mask and *fins*. Then he dove into the water.

CLUE: The words *dove into the water* tell you where the diver went. This phrase tells you that *fins* are something useful that a person can wear in water.

Using the context is a good way to understand the meaning of a new word. Here is another strategy for using context clues to understand the word *caverns* from the essay on page 28.

Read the sentence with the unknown word and some of the sentences around it.

*This created **caverns** deep in the earth.*

Look for context clues. What details about **The Location or Setting** can you find?

Caverns are found below the earth's surface.

Think about the context clues and other information you may already know.

Caves can also be found below the earth's surface.

Predict a meaning for the word.

A *cavern* must be a large cave or hollow area under the earth's surface.

Check the Word Wisdom Dictionary to be sure of the meaning.

The word *cavern* means "a very large cave."

Unlock the Meanings

Practice the Strategy Here is one of the boldfaced words from the essay on page 28. Use the context clues strategy on page 29 to figure out the meaning of this word.

crater

Read the sentence that uses the word *crater* and some of the sentences around it.

Look for context clues. What details about **The Location or Setting** can you find?

_____

_____

_____

Think about the context clues. What other helpful information do you know?

_____

_____

_____

Predict a meaning for the word *crater*.

_____

_____

_____

Check the Word Wisdom Dictionary to be sure of the meaning of the word *crater*.

_____

_____

_____

	WORD LIST
	meteorite
	peninsula
✔	crater
	disaster
	limestone
✔	cavern
	sinkhole
	archaeologist
	aquatic
	fossil

Use Context Clues You have been introduced to two of the words from the essay on page 28. These words have been checked off on the Word List. In the first column, write the other eight words from the Word List. In the second column, predict a meaning for each word using context clues. Then look up the meaning in your Word Wisdom Dictionary. In the third column, write the dictionary meaning that fits the context.

	Vocabulary Word	Your Prediction	Dictionary Says
1			
2			
3			
4			
5			
6			
7			
8			

Process the Meanings

WORD LIST

- meteorite
- peninsula
- crater
- disaster
- limestone
- cavern
- sinkhole
- archaeologist
- aquatic
- fossil

Use the Words Correctly in Writing Rewrite each sentence in your own words. Include the word in parentheses in your sentence.

1 When the middle of my street collapsed, we suddenly had a caved-in place in our neighborhood. (sinkhole)

_____

2 My sister loves to do water ballet in a swimming pool. (aquatic)

_____

3 Florida is a landmass that sticks out into the water. (peninsula)

_____

4 Taking care of a two-year-old can turn into a big mess. (disaster)

_____

Match the Meanings Write the vocabulary word from the Word List that matches each meaning.

Meaning	Vocabulary Word
5 an ancient trace of a plant or an animal	_____
6 a person who studies the past through old objects or remains	_____
7 a type of soft rock	_____
8 solid matter that falls from space	_____
9 a very large cave	_____
10 a bowl-shaped dent in the earth's surface	_____

✎ Apply What You've Learned

Relate the Meanings Use what you've learned about the boldfaced words to answer the questions.

1 How could a **meteorite** create a **disaster**?

_____

_____

2 What kind of **fossil** might an **archaeologist** find?

_____

_____

3 What might live in an **aquatic cavern**?

_____

_____

4 How is a **crater** like a **sinkhole**?

_____

_____

5 How can a **peninsula** be made of **limestone?**

_____

_____

 Write It! Write a paragraph about something you once discovered (or would like to discover) in the earth or in a body of water. Use as many vocabulary words from Part 1 as you can.

Latin and Greek Roots

for Word Wisdom

A "Rocky" Interview:

The Surprise From Space

Here is an interview with Penny Baker. She discovered something special in her own backyard.

Interviewer: Hello Ms. Baker. How did you happen to find this **asteroid**?

Penny Baker: Well, I didn't really find it by myself. Some city workers spotted it first. They were digging an **aqueduct** behind my house. It will carry water to the new Bedford Hills development. The aqueduct is near the back edge of our property.

Interviewer: Do they always build aqueducts so close to houses?

Penny Baker: No, but they had to do it because of the **geography** around here. With all of the hills, most of the ground is rocky. Some of it is solid rock. The ground near our house isn't very rocky. It was the best place for the aqueduct.

Interviewer: That makes sense. How deep was the **cavity** where you found the asteroid?

Penny Baker: The crew had just started to **excavate** the ground. The hole was about four feet deep. I was watching them work from my kitchen window. When I saw the crew pointing into the hole, I went out to look. I could see tiny bits of colors in the rock, including yellow, dark blue, and **aquamarine**.

Interviewer: How did you know it was an asteroid? Are you a trained **geologist**?

Penny Baker: No, but I am very interested in **astronomy**. I know quite a bit about the stars and the planets. When I was little, I wanted to be an **astronaut**. But later, I decided to be a teacher. My current students are learning a lot about the stars. Some teachers at school choose to have an **aquarium,** but I have stars and planets hanging from our classroom ceiling.

Interviewer: So you knew it was an asteroid. What happened next?

Penny Baker: The workers dug the asteroid out of the soil. It was as big as a cantaloupe! I called the local college and asked for the astronomy department. A woman there told me she would be right over. She pulled into my driveway about ten minutes later. She was very excited!

Interviewer: I can see why! You made quite a discovery. Thanks for talking to us today.

Practice the Context Clues Strategy   Here is one of the boldfaced words from the interview on page 34. Use the context clues strategy you learned in Part 1 on page 29 to figure out the meaning of this word.

excavate

📖 **Read** the sentence that uses the word *excavate* and some of the sentences around it.

🔍 **Look** for context clues to the word's meaning. What details about **The Location or Setting** can you find?

_____

_____

_____

💡 **Think** about the context clues. What other helpful information do you know?

_____

_____

_____

➡️ **Predict** a meaning for the word *excavate*.

_____

_____

✔️ **Check** your Word Wisdom Dictionary to be sure of the meaning of the word *excavate*. Write the definition here.

_____

_____

Unlock the Meanings

Many English words come from Latin or Greek roots. If you know the meaning of different roots, you can often unlock the meaning of many new words. The following roots relate to the earth.

Latin Root: **cav**
meaning: hollow
English word: *cavern*
meaning: a very large cave

Greek Root: **astr**
meaning: star
English word: *astronomer*
meaning: one who studies stars and planets

Latin Root: **aqua**
meaning: water
English word: *aquatic*
meaning: relating to water

Greek Root: **geo**
meaning: earth
English word: *geology*
meaning: the study of the earth

Sort by Roots Find these roots in the Word List. Write each word on a line under the correct root. Think of other words that come from the same Latin and Greek roots. Write each word in the correct place.

WORD LIST

| asteroid |
| aqueduct |
| geography |
| cavity |
| excavate |
| aquamarine |
| geologist |
| astronomy |
| astronaut |
| aquarium |

Latin Root:
cav

_____

_____

_____

_____

Greek Root:
astr

_____

_____

_____

_____

Latin Root:
aqua

_____

_____

_____

_____

Greek Root:
geo

_____

_____

_____

_____

The Earth

Prefix	Meaning
ex-	out of, from

Example

ex- (from) + cav (hollow) + -ate (verb) = excavate

Use Roots and Prefixes Circle any roots and prefixes you find in the boldfaced words below. Use context clues, roots, and prefixes to write the meaning of the word. Check your definitions in the Word Wisdom Dictionary.

1 The planetarium is a good place to study **astronomy**.

_____

2 The dentist will fill the small **cavity** in my tooth.

_____

3 Maria has a collection of rocks; she wants to be a **geologist**.

_____

4 The city **aqueduct** carries water to the next county.

_____

5 I am interested in **geography** because I like to study different places.

_____

6 Add water to the **aquarium** or the fish will die.

_____

7 Allie's eyes are **aquamarine**, like water in a pool.

_____

8 My brother wants to **excavate** the yard to look for treasure.

_____

9 Would you like to be an **astronaut** and fly around in space?

_____

10 I saw a movie about an **asteroid** that almost hit the earth.

_____

Process the Meanings

WORD LIST

WORD LIST

asteroid

aqueduct

geography

cavity

excavate

aquamarine

geologist

astronomy

astronaut

aquarium

Choose the Correct Word Circle the boldfaced word that completes each sentence correctly.

1 My class is learning about the **asteroids/astronomy** that revolve around the sun.

2 Lee's bedroom is **aquamarine/aqueduct**, like the sea.

3 A mouse lived in the **cavity/cavern** by the door.

4 My uncle studies the stars. He enjoys **asteroid/astronomy**.

5 The **aquarium/aqueduct** no longer carries water into town.

Use the Clues Use the clues to complete each "Help Wanted" sign. Write the missing words.

6 A miner is needed to _____ dirt and rocks from a cavern.

7 A _____ is needed to help a museum

organize a collection of rocks.

8 Someone is needed to take care of an _____.

The person must have knowledge of fish and aquatic

plants.

9 An _____ is needed to fly a spacecraft.

The person must like small spaces and far-off places.

10 An explorer is needed to discover new lands. The person

must have a good understanding of _____.

Apply What You've Learned

Demonstrate Word Knowledge   Answer the questions.

1 What do you do when you have a **cavity**?

_____

2 What might you put in an **aquarium**? Discuss three items.

_____

3 What is the **geography** of the area in which you live?

_____

4 Why are **aqueducts** important to modern life?

_____

5 Would you stand out in a pool wearing **aquamarine**? Explain.

_____

6 In what class are you likely to study **asteroids**?

_____

7 What would you imagine that an **astronaut** would need?

_____

8 What tools might a **geologist** need?

_____

9 Why might someone want to study **astronomy**?

_____

10 Where would you like to **excavate** and why?

_____

Speak It!   Create a radio "Help Wanted" ad like those on page 38. Use as many vocabulary words from Part 2 as you can. Perform your radio ad for the class.

Reference Skills

for Word Wisdom

Blowing Smoke:

Volcanoes and Our Health

Volcanoes are powerful forces. They not only change the shape of the land. They also change the air we breathe— and not for the better.

Have you ever seen a volcano erupt? First, **tremors** shake the Earth. Then the volcano explodes. Gases shoot high into the **atmosphere**. A volcano called Kilauea has been erupting since 1983. Kilauea is in Hawaii. Every day, it sends about 2,000 tons of sulfur dioxide gas into the air. The gas comes from magma inside the volcano. During an **eruption,** the gas bubbles out of the magma. It mixes with the air.

Sulfur dioxide is harmful. In the air, it combines with oxygen, dust, and moisture. Sunlight warms it. The result is volcanic smog, or vog. Vog **pollutes** the air. It becomes harder to see and breathe. Vog gives people headaches and sore throats. Their eyes water. Even driving through vog is hard. Drivers have to use their headlights even during the day.

Vog also hurts crops. It causes acid rain. This rain can burn plants growing in fields and **ravines**. Vog even slips into greenhouses through air vents.

Many Hawaiians catch rainwater on their rooftops. Unfortunately, they drink the water from these **reservoirs**. Acid rain from the volcano has polluted this water. It is not safe to drink.

Experts in **meteorology** have studied the winds around Kilauea. The Hawaiian Islands are close together. Only **straits** of water separate them. Thus, winds spread Kilauea's vog to the other islands. In fact, traces of vog have been found 1,000 miles away!

Other volcanoes also pollute the air. Nearly every continent on Earth has volcanoes. There are no **stellar** volcanoes, as stars are made of burning gases. Still, there are volcanoes on other planets. This includes Mars and Venus. Long ago, there were volcanoes on the moon. They erupted billions of years ago. These **lunar** volcanoes produced magma. The magma cooled and became lava. The lava spread over most of the moon's surface.

We still have much to learn about volcanoes. We cannot predict when they will erupt. Yet, we are learning more about them every day. We cannot control volcanoes, so we must learn how to deal with them.

Practice the Context Clues Strategy   Here is one of the boldfaced words from the selection on page 40. Use the context clues strategy you learned in Part 1 on page 29 to figure out the meaning of this word.

strait

📖 **Read** the sentence that uses the word *strait* and some of the sentences around it.

🔍 **Look** for context clues to the word's meaning. What details about **The Location or Setting** can you find?

_____

_____

_____

💡 **Think** about the context clues. What other helpful information do you know?

_____

_____

_____

➤ **Predict** a meaning for the word *strait*.

_____

_____

✔ **Check** your Word Wisdom Dictionary to be sure of the meaning of the word *strait*. Which of the meanings for the word *strait* fits the context?

_____

_____

Unlock the Meanings

Guide words help you find words in a dictionary. They appear at the top of every dictionary page. The first guide word shows the *first* dictionary entry on the page. The second guide word shows the *last* dictionary entry on the same page. The word you are looking for will appear in alphabetical order between the two guide words.

Guide Words

assortment   astronaut

The word *asteroid* would appear on the same page as these guide words. It comes between them in alphabetical order.

Use Guide Words Here are pairs of guide words that appear at the top of a dictionary page. Find the words from the Word List on the next page that would appear on each dictionary page.

matter, mount

1 _____

rabbit, round

2 _____

3 _____

stand, street

4 _____

5 _____

llama, lunch

6 _____

trek, trench

7 _____

atlas, atom

8 _____

poll, polo

9 _____

error, essay

10 _____

Find the Meaning
1. Use context clues.
2. Look for a familiar root, prefix, or suffix.
3. If the context or a word part doesn't help, check the dictionary.

Define the Words   Follow the steps above to write the meaning of each boldfaced word. Write 1, 2, or 3 to show which steps you used.

WORD LIST

tremor
atmosphere
eruption
pollute
ravine
reservoir
meteorology
strait
stellar
lunar

1 The lead actor gave a **stellar** performance.

_____

2 I would be afraid during the **eruption** of a volcano.

_____

3 The sailors could see land on both sides of the narrow **strait**.

_____

4 The water in the **reservoir** was high after the heavy rains.

_____

5 Study **meteorology** if you want to forecast the weather.

_____

6 Months on a **lunar** calendar are based on the moon.

_____

7 The earth's **atmosphere** has oxygen and other gases.

_____

8 If we **pollute** our air and water, we will not be healthy.

_____

9 I felt the earthquake when a **tremor** woke me up.

_____

10 The stream rushed down the **ravine** between the two hillsides.

_____

Process the Meanings

WORD LIST

- tremor
- atmosphere
- eruption
- pollute
- ravine
- reservoir
- meteorology
- strait
- stellar
- lunar

Choose the Correct Word   Write the word from the Word List that best matches each definition.

1 a place where water is stored: _____

2 to dirty the air, land, or water: _____

3 a sudden explosion: _____

4 the air surrounding something: _____

5 a narrow valley: _____

Complete the Analogies   Complete each analogy with a word from the Word List.

6 A hallway is to a gym as a _____ is to an ocean.

7 Chills are to a cold as a _____ is to an earthquake.

8 Aquatic is to water as _____ is to stars.

9 Astronomy is to space as _____ is to weather.

10 Martian is to Mars as _____ is to moon.

11 Money is to wallet as water is to _____.

12 Narrow is to _____ as tall is to mountain.

13 _____ is to volcano as blast is to dynamite.

14 Clean is to _____ as sleep is to work.

15 Space is to Earth as _____ is to ground.

Apply What You've Learned

Relate the Meanings Answer each question or respond to each statement.

1 What might cause an **eruption** of happiness from someone?

_____

2 Describe the **atmosphere** at a party you once attended.

_____

3 When might a baby sitter need a **reservoir** of patience?

_____

4 How would you feel about a **polluted** stream nearby?

_____

5 When might you feel a **tremor**?

_____

6 What should a person do if he or she gets lost in a **ravine**?

_____

Complete the Sentences Complete each sentence.

7 People who study **meteorology** _____

8 A **stellar** night sky _____

9 You could cross a **strait** more quickly than an ocean because

_____

10 Upon a **lunar** landing, astronauts might see _____

_____

Write It! What interests you most about the earth? Tell why in a paragraph. Use as many words from Part 3 as you can.

WORD LIST

- meteorite
- peninsula
- crater
- disaster
- limestone
- cavern
- sinkhole
- archaeologist
- aquatic
- fossil
- asteroid
- aqueduct
- geography
- cavity
- excavate
- aquamarine
- geologist
- astronomy
- astronaut
- aquarium
- tremor
- atmosphere
- eruption
- pollute
- ravine
- reservoir
- meteorology
- strait
- stellar
- lunar

Review (for Word Wisdom)

Sort by Meanings Decide whether each word is most closely related to land, sky, or water. Write the word in the column with the related meaning. A few words do not belong in any of the groups.

Land Words	Sky Words	Water Words

Find Related Words Read the sentences. Look at the underlined word part. Write the word from the Word List that contains the underlined word part *and* fits the context.

1 The boy was <u>rav</u>enous after being lost in a

_____ for two days.

2 We felt a <u>trem</u>endous _____ during the earthquake.

3 The water in the <u>aqu</u>arium was _____.

4 Miners ex<u>cav</u>ated coal from the _____.

5 The <u>astro</u>naut took a course in _____.

Check the Meanings If the boldfaced word is used correctly, write **C**. If the word is used incorrectly, write **I**. Tell a partner how you would fix the incorrect items.

____ **6** My sister has curly hair, but my hair is **strait.**

____ **7** Because Omar is a good runner, he has won awards for his **aquatic** ability.

____ **8** **Meteorology** is the study of weather.

____ **9** Alex is learning how to paint in his **geography** class.

____ **10** Our supermarket gets juice through an **aqueduct.**

____ **11** **Lunar** rocks are on the moon.

____ **12** Don't **pollute** the ground with trash.

____ **13** The **cavity** rose up out of the earth.

____ **14** The **geologist** found a layer of buried rock.

____ **15** **Archaeologists** design buildings.

Taking Vocabulary Tests

TEST-TAKING STRATEGY

If you have trouble answering a multiple-choice question, first eliminate any answers that you know are wrong. Then decide among the remaining answer choices. This improves your chance of choosing the correct one.

Sample:

a calm <u>strait</u>
- Ⓐ water channel
- Ⓑ mountain view
- Ⓒ cloudy sky
- Ⓓ star constellation

Practice Test   Fill in the letter of the answer choice that shows the correct meaning for the underlined word.

1 a small <u>eruption</u>
- Ⓐ mix-up
- Ⓑ delay
- Ⓒ volcano
- Ⓓ explosion

2 an experienced <u>astronaut</u>
- Ⓐ person who explores space
- Ⓑ person who rides horses
- Ⓒ person who tells fortunes
- Ⓓ person who dives

3 an empty <u>reservoir</u>
- Ⓐ nest
- Ⓑ promise
- Ⓒ place to sit
- Ⓓ place for storage

4 a famous <u>geologist</u>
- Ⓐ person who studies the stars
- Ⓑ person who studies the earth
- Ⓒ person who is good at math
- Ⓓ person who makes maps

5 a small <u>cavity</u>
- Ⓐ tooth
- Ⓑ pain
- Ⓒ hole
- Ⓓ hill

6 to <u>pollute</u> the ocean
- Ⓐ dirty
- Ⓑ clean
- Ⓒ live in
- Ⓓ drive around

7 a <u>stellar</u> performance
- Ⓐ stage
- Ⓑ star
- Ⓒ poor
- Ⓓ repeat

8 a <u>lunar</u> vehicle
- Ⓐ space
- Ⓑ sun
- Ⓒ moon
- Ⓓ broken

9 an <u>aquatic</u> plant
- Ⓐ green
- Ⓑ found in air
- Ⓒ found in water
- Ⓓ house

10 a sudden <u>disaster</u>
- Ⓐ phone call
- Ⓑ tragedy
- Ⓒ idea
- Ⓓ movement

crater   peninsula   meteorite   sinkhole   fossil
disaster   limestone   aquarium   excavate   geologist
aquamarine asteroid   aqueduct   atmosphere eruption
pollute   tremor   stellar   lunar   reservoir

Solve the Word Puzzle   Look at the vocabulary words in the box. Choose a word to fit each meaning below. Write one letter on each line. Then complete the sentence in the bottom box by copying the circled letters onto the lines in the box.

1 a layer of air surrounding the earth:

—— —— —— ——(——)(——) —— —— —— ——

2 to dig out: (——)—— —— —— —— —— —— ——

3 related to the moon: (——)(——)(——)—— ——

4 a collapsed place: —— —— ——(——)—— —— —— ——

5 a dent made by a meteorite: —— —— —— ——(——)(——)

A person who likes to explore caves is a

—— —— —— —— —— —— —— —— —— ——.

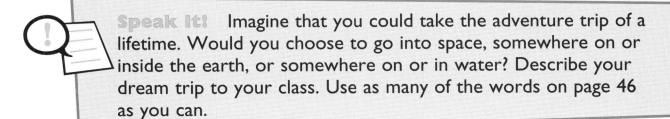

Speak It!   Imagine that you could take the adventure trip of a lifetime. Would you choose to go into space, somewhere on or inside the earth, or somewhere on or in water? Describe your dream trip to your class. Use as many of the words on page 46 as you can.

Context Clues

for Word Wisdom

Then and Now:
Medicine

The practice of medicine has changed over time. So have the ways in which people take care of their bodies. Read about some health practices that are different today from the way they used to be.

Today we think of barbers as people who cut men's hair. However, barbers in the past did much more serious cutting. They did the work of **surgeons,** performing operations and cutting out diseased organs. They also did the work of dentists, pulling out rotten teeth. In the Middle Ages, people believed that **infections** were caused by "bad blood." To cure these diseases, barbers used bloodletting, a medical **remedy** in which leeches sucked blood from a patient's veins.

As you can imagine, people didn't go to a barber for something like a **manicure** or a **pedicure**. Beauty and skin-care treatments for hands or for feet were not what barbers did when they weren't cutting hair or beards. They were performing life-and-death medical procedures instead.

For a long time, people knew nothing about **germs**. In the 1800s, the French scientist Louis Pasteur showed that those tiny living things spread disease. Until Pasteur, people also didn't know

the importance of cleanliness. It took years before barbers or doctors even washed their hands before they **examined** and then treated the next patient.

Another of Pasteur's great contributions to medicine was his recognition of the importance of **vaccines,** which can prevent many illnesses. Today **physicians** often inject healthy patients with these substances, which contain weakened germs.

Much more has changed since Pasteur's time. Interestingly enough, some of the old practices are being used again. Doctors have found that leeches may help patients recover from surgery. Many people today also use some of the **herbs** that were so popular in the past. Plant parts are used by themselves to cure certain problems, or they are used along with other medical treatments.

What about medicine in the future? It seems likely that many things will change while others will remain the same.

Health

UNIT

3

Context Clues Strategy

Look for What the Word Is Used For

EXAMPLE: The dentist took *x-rays* to check Jay's teeth for hidden cavities.

CLUE: The words *to check Jay's teeth for hidden cavities* explain what *x-rays* are used for.

Here are steps to figure out the meaning of the word *remedy*, which appears in the essay about medicine.

Read the sentence with the unknown word and some of the sentences around it.

*To cure these diseases, barbers used bloodletting, a medical **remedy** in which leeches sucked blood from a patient's veins.*

Look for context clues. What words can you find that tell **What the Word Is Used For?**

The words *to cure these diseases* tell that a *remedy* was used for curing people.

Think about the context clues and other helpful information you may already know.

My mom says that chicken soup is a *remedy* for a bad cold. It makes me feel better when I'm sick.

Predict a meaning for the word.

A *remedy* is probably a "cure for something."

Check the Word Wisdom Dictionary to be sure of the meaning. Decide which of the meanings in the dictionary fits the context.

The word *remedy* means "something that relieves pain."

Practice the Strategy   Here is another boldfaced word from the essay about medicine on page 50. Use the context clues strategy on page 51 to figure out the meaning of the word.

vaccines

Read the sentence that uses the word *vaccines* and some of the sentences around it.

Look for context clues to the word's meaning. What words can you find that tell **What the Word Is Used For?**

_____

_____

_____

Think about the context clues and other helpful information you may already know.

_____

_____

_____

Predict a meaning for the word *vaccines*.

_____

_____

_____

Check your Word Wisdom Dictionary to be sure of the meaning of the word *vaccine*. Write the dictionary definition.

_____

_____

_____

Use Context Clues The two words you have learned so far are checked off in the Word List. Write the other eight words from the Word List in the first column. Use context clues to predict a meaning for each word under "Your Prediction." Check the meanings in the Word Wisdom Dictionary. Write the definition under "Dictionary Says."

WORD LIST

surgeon
infection
✔ remedy
manicure
pedicure
germ
examine
✔ vaccine
physician
herb

Vocabulary Word	Your Prediction	Dictionary Says
1		
2		
3		
4		
5		
6		
7		
8		

Process the Meanings

WORD LIST

surgeon
infection
remedy
manicure
pedicure
germ
examine
vaccine
physician
herb

Use the Words Correctly in Writing Rewrite each sentence in your own words. Include the word in parentheses in your sentence. You may add a new ending to the word.

1 My mother uses parts of a plant to improve her memory. (herb)

_____

2 Be sure to clean a cut so you don't get an illness. (infection)

_____

3 The doctor gave me a substance with weakened disease germs so that I won't get measles. (vaccine)

_____

4 Have you ever had a beauty treatment for your feet and toenails? (pedicure)

_____

5 The doctor will look closely at your throat to see why it is sore. (examine)

_____

Match the Definitions Write the word from the column on the right that matches each definition.

6 tiny living thing   _____   remedy
that causes illness

7 cure   _____   manicure

8 doctor who performs _____   surgeon
operations

9 beauty treatment for _____   germ
hands and nails

10 medical doctor   _____   physician

Apply What You've Learned

Relate the Meanings Answer the questions. Use the boldfaced words in your answers.

1 How can a **surgeon** prevent an **infection**?

_____

_____

2 Why would a **physician** give someone a **vaccine**?

_____

_____

3 When would someone receiving a **pedicure** want to **examine** his or her feet?

_____

_____

4 How could a person giving a **manicure** keep from spreading **germs**?

_____

_____

5 For what might a person use an **herb** as a **remedy**?

_____

_____

Write It! Would you like to be a medical doctor when you grow up? Write about the special skills a medical doctor might need and whether you would like to learn those skills. Use as many words as you can from the Word List on page 54.

Latin and Greek Roots

for Word Wisdom

Healthy Feet Are Happy Feet:

Feet and Fashion

Do you know any people who have problems with their feet? Many do. Aching feet make standing and walking painful. Why do so many feet hurt?

A **podiatrist** named Simon J. Wikler explained the history of foot problems. Long ago, people had healthy feet. Back then, they used **manual** labor to get things done. Workers either went barefoot or they wore sensible shoes that protected their feet.

At that time, working people were **pedestrians**. They walked wherever they needed to go in their flat, plain shoes. The lucky ones had bicycles and pushed the **pedals** with their plain, unstylish shoes. Wealthy people rode in carriages and rarely walked. They paid others to do their work. Many wore stylish shoes with high heels and pointed toes. Some workers admired rich people and put them on **pedestals**. They gazed at their fancy shoes with **affection**. The workers longed for the day when they could afford to be stylish.

With the Industrial Revolution, people began to use machines to do their work. Workers had more money and did less manual labor. They wanted stylish shoes. Shoemakers rushed to **manufacture** these shoes. New machinery made them easier and cheaper to produce. Soon many people could afford stylish shoes.

The front of these shoes was shaped to a sharp point. The wearer's toes were squashed together. The shoes were like **manacles,** but instead of confining people's hands, they confined their feet. However, no one noticed the **defects** in these shoes. Instead, they forced themselves to stand and walk in them. In spite of the pain, they beamed happily. Their **facial** expressions showed their pride in their shoes.

Soon millions of people had crippled feet. Fortunately, in the 1930s people wanted a more modern look. It was the Jazz Age, and people wanted comfortable shoes suitable for dancing. The toes of shoes became broader, and the heels became shorter.

But beware! Popular styles change. Don't sacrifice your feet to fashion!

Practice the Context Clues Strategy Here is one of the boldfaced words from the essay on page 56. Use the context clues strategy you learned in Part 1 on page 51 to figure out the meaning of this word.

manacles

📖 **Read** the sentence that uses the word *manacles* and some of the sentences around it.

🔍 **Look** for context clues to the word's meaning. What words can you find that tell **What the Word Is Used For?**

_____

_____

_____

💡 **Think** about the context clues. What other helpful information do you know?

_____

_____

_____

➡️ **Predict** a meaning for the word *manacle*.

_____

_____

_____

✅ **Check** your Word Wisdom Dictionary to be sure of the meaning of the word *manacle*. Which of the meanings for the word *manacle* fits the context?

_____

_____

_____

Unlock the Meanings

Knowing the meanings of Latin and Greek roots can help you figure out the meanings of new words. Several words you learned in Part 1 have a Latin or Greek root. Each root relates to health.

Latin Root: **manu**
meaning: hand
English word: *manicure*
meaning: a treatment for hands and fingernails

Latin and Greek Root: **ped, pod**
meaning: foot
English word: *pedicure*
meaning: a treatment for feet and toenails

Latin Root: **fac, fect, fic**
meaning: to make; to do; easy; face
English word: *infection*
meaning: an illness caused by germs

WORD LIST

podiatrist
manual
pedestrian
pedal
pedestal
affection
manufacture
manacle
defect
facial

Sort by Roots Find these roots in the Word List. Write each word on a line below the correct root. Remember that the spellings of roots can change. Think of other words that come from the same Latin or Greek roots. Write each word in the correct column.

Latin Root: **manu**

Latin and Greek Root: **ped, pod**

Latin Root: **fac, fect, fic**

_____   _____   _____

_____   _____   _____

_____   _____   _____

_____   _____   _____

_____   _____   _____

Health

Prefix	Meaning
de-	opposite of

Example

de- (opposite of) + fect (to do) = defect

Use Roots and Prefixes Circle the root and any prefix you find in the boldfaced words below. Use context clues, roots, and prefixes to write the meaning of each boldfaced word. Check your definitions in a dictionary.

1 The **podiatrist** said I needed special shoes to reduce foot pain.

_____

2 Don's cat shows **affection** by rubbing Don's ear with her nose.

_____

3 Becky has a new bike, but her feet don't reach the **pedals**.

_____

4 Wear a bike helmet so you don't get any head or **facial** injuries.

_____

5 The prisoner's hands were locked in **manacles**.

_____

6 We have a leaf blower, but I prefer the **manual** task of raking leaves.

_____

7 Is there a bump on my nose, or does that mirror have a **defect**?

_____

8 The famous statue is on a **pedestal**, so you'll be able to see it easily.

_____

9 Early New England mills **manufactured** shoes and woolens.

_____

10 Main Street has a narrow lane for **pedestrians** to walk safely.

_____

WORD LIST

- podiatrist
- manual
- pedestrian
- pedal
- pedestal
- affection
- manufacture
- manacle
- defect
- facial

Complete the Paragraph Fill in each blank with a word from the Word List. You may add an ending to some words.

Pablo is a sculptor who makes statues of people. He likes to use tools that are **1** _____ by a company that is fifty years old. Pablo enjoys **2** _____ work better than using machines. The statues' faces are special because he works hard sculpting each person's unique **3** _____ features. Pablo spends so much time with his statues that they seem like family members. He has great **4** _____ for all of the statues, even the ones with small mistakes, or **5** _____.

He proudly places each of his completed statues on a **6** _____.

Choose the Correct Word Write the word that best completes each sentence. Choose words from the Word List that you didn't use above. Add a plural ending if it is needed.

7 On Sundays, no cars are allowed in the park; only _____ may enter.

8 You need a special key to unlock a pair of _____.

9 You might want a _____ to look at your sore toe.

10 In earlier times, bicycle riders kicked their feet along the road because the bikes did not have _____.

Demonstrate Word Knowledge Answer the questions or follow the directions.

1 What would you use to wash dishes using the **manual** method?

_____

2 Name some things you might put on a **pedestal**.

_____

3 Name three things that are **manufactured**.

_____

4 When might a person need a **podiatrist**?

_____

5 Describe which of your **facial** features you like best.

_____

Complete the Sentences Write an answer that completes each sentence.

6 A person might wear a **manacle** if _____

7 A person might show **affection** by _____

8 If something you bought had a **defect**, you might _____

_____

9 Two places you might find a **pedal** are _____

10 If you are a **pedestrian**, you _____

Speak It! Suppose you manufacture robots that look like humans. Tell your class about your factory. Use as many words as you can from the Word List on page 60.

Reference Skills

for Word Wisdom

Bubonic Plague:

The Black Death

In the 1340s, a plague began in China. It quickly spread across Asia. By 1346, more than twenty-three million people had died. In 1347, the plague reached Italy. It followed trade routes throughout Europe. In some cities, six of every ten people died.

This **epidemic** included three kinds of plague. All were very **contagious**. In one kind, the victims had swollen glands. They were **feverish** and had headaches and aching joints. Another kind affected the lungs. The most **toxic** kind caused spots on the patient's skin to turn black. These black spots gave the epidemic its name, the Black Death.

Bacteria caused all three kinds of plague. Rats carried two kinds of the disease. When fleas bit the rats, the fleas became carriers. When the fleas bit people, the people quickly became sick. Droplets of water spread the third kind of plague when an infected person coughed. The victims often died on the first day they showed symptoms. These three diseases killed thirty to one hundred percent of their victims. No one was **immune** to them. Even strong people with no **frailty** died within a few days.

People did not know what caused this set of diseases. They burned incense to cover up the smell of people dying. They rang church bells to drive the plague away. They blamed the epidemic on earthquakes and movements of the stars. They did not realize that rats and fleas carried the disease or that bacteria existed. They did not wash their hands before they prepared food or ate. Their kitchens and homes were not **sanitary**.

Back then, doctors could not even **diagnose** the plague. Today, they can write a **prescription** that will cure two kinds of the disease. The most toxic kind still has no treatment. Fortunately, it is very rare.

Medicine has come a long way since the 1340s. Now we understand how bacteria can make us sick. Still, we have much to learn about cancers and other illnesses. Six hundred years from now, people will probably be amazed at what we don't know now!

Practice the Context Clues Strategy   Here is one of the boldfaced words from the essay on page 62. Use the context clues strategy you learned in Part 1 on page 51 to figure out the meaning of this word.

prescription

Read the sentence that uses the word *prescription* and some of the sentences around it.

Look for context clues to the word's meaning. What words can you find that tell **What the Word Is Used For?**

_____

_____

Think about the context clues. What other helpful information do you know?

_____

_____

_____

Predict a meaning for the word *prescription*.

_____

_____

_____

Check your Word Wisdom Dictionary to be sure of the meaning of the word *prescription*. Write the definition here.

_____

_____

_____

Unlock the Meanings

The Encyclopedia An encyclopedia is a good source of information when you want to learn more about a topic. The articles in an encyclopedia are arranged in alphabetical order. To find an article, identify a key word for your topic, such as "disease." Look in the volume that includes the topic. You might also find cross-references that list additional topics you can explore. An example for the topic "disease" is shown here.

> **Disease.**
> See *also* **Contagious disease; Communicable disease; Infectious disease**

Choose the Key Words Decide which word or words in each topic are useful key words to help you find an encyclopedia article. Write your answer on the line.

Topic	Key Word
1 kinds of bacteria	
2 how an epidemic spreads	
3 a history of the microscope	
4 careers in nursing	
5 the causes of pneumonia	
6 how doctors diagnose disease	
7 chemicals that are toxins	
8 side effects of a fever	
9 how pharmacists keep track of prescriptions	
10 the body's immune system	

Find the Meaning

1. Use context clues.
2. Look for a familiar root, prefix, or suffix.
3. If the context or a word part doesn't help, check the dictionary.

Define the Words Follow the steps above to write the meaning of each boldfaced word. Write 1, 2, or 3 to show which steps you used.

1 Wash your hands to kill **bacteria** that could make you sick.

_____

2 A doctor may give you a **prescription** for medicine.

_____

3 If you have a **contagious** disease, stay away from healthy people.

_____

4 The boy felt **feverish**, so he stayed home from school.

_____

5 Wearing clean socks every day is a **sanitary** habit.

_____

6 Even medicine can be **toxic** if you take too much.

_____

7 There's no sign of **frailty** in Grandmother; she swims a mile a day!

_____

8 The flu **epidemic** spread quickly around the world.

_____

9 The doctor did some tests to **diagnose** my illness.

_____

10 Once you have chicken pox, you usually become **immune**.

_____

WORD LIST

epidemic
contagious
feverish
toxic
bacteria
immune
frailty
sanitary
diagnose
prescription

WORD LIST

epidemic

contagious

feverish

toxic

bacteria

immune

frailty

sanitary

diagnose

prescription

Complete the Analogies Complete each analogy with a word from the Word List.

1 Happy is to sad as frozen is to _____.

2 Medicine is to healthful as poison is to

_____.

3 Medical doctor is to physician as germs is to

_____.

4 Parent is to permission slip as doctor is to

_____.

Match the Word and Meaning Write the letter of the definition next to the word it defines.

_____ **5** diagnose

_____ **6** frailty

_____ **7** sanitary

_____ **8** epidemic

_____ **9** contagious

_____ **10** immune

a. capable of spreading disease from one person to another

b. determine the cause

c. free of germs

d. protected from illness

e. weakness

f. disease that spreads widely and quickly

Apply What You've Learned

Relate the Meanings Answer each question.

1 How might you avoid getting a **contagious** disease?

_____

2 How might a doctor **diagnose** a problem you are having?

_____

3 How might people find out about an **epidemic**?

_____

4 What is one way you could become **immune** to a disease?

_____

5 When might you need a **prescription**?

_____

Complete the Sentences Complete each sentence below.

6 You might find harmful **bacteria** in _____

_____

7 If you are **feverish,** you should _____

_____

8 Avoid **toxic** plants because _____

_____

9 One sign of **frailty** is _____

10 You could make a place **sanitary** by _____

_____

Write It! Write a short health handbook for children. Write five or more tips in complete sentences. Use several words from the Word List on page 66.

WORD LIST

surgeon
infection
remedy
manicure
pedicure
germ
examine
vaccine
physician
herb
podiatrist
manual
pedestrian
pedal
pedestal
affection
manufacture
manacle
defect
facial
epidemic
contagious
feverish
toxic
bacteria
immune
frailty
sanitary
diagnose
prescription

Review
for Word Wisdom

Sort by Types of Words   Decide whether each word in the Word List tells about something that is mostly helpful, mostly harmful, or neither helpful nor harmful. Write the word under the best heading.

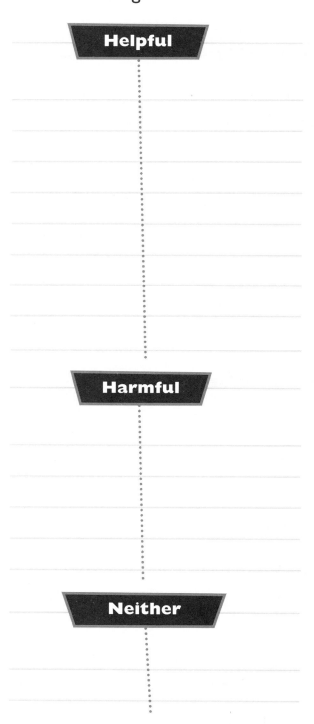

Helpful

Harmful

Neither

Demonstrate Word Knowledge Follow the directions by using vocabulary words. Do not repeat a word.

1 Name three people who could write a prescription.

_____

2 Name three things that could cause disease.

_____

3 Name two things that could prevent or cure a disease.

_____

4 Name two reasons why diseases are spread.

_____

5 Name two things people might have done to their nails.

_____

Follow the Directions Answer each question.

6 When might people use **herbs**? _____

_____

7 What is something that is **toxic**? _____

_____

8 Why should you not worry if you are **immune** to a disease?

_____

9 Where would you see a **pedestrian**? _____

_____

10 What are some items in your school that are **manufactured**?

_____

Taking Vocabulary Tests

Practice Test   Fill in the circle of the answer that gives the correct meaning of the underlined word.

1 sign of frailty
Ⓐ weakness
Ⓑ friendship
Ⓒ hunger
Ⓓ anger

2 examine the kitten
Ⓐ pet
Ⓑ hold
Ⓒ check
Ⓓ visit

3 with manual controls
Ⓐ automatic
Ⓑ handmade
Ⓒ easily changed
Ⓓ operated by hand

4 feverish child
Ⓐ having a pleasant dream
Ⓑ having a high temperature
Ⓒ having a temper tantrum
Ⓓ having a wonderful friend

5 diagnose an illness
Ⓐ get
Ⓑ cure
Ⓒ avoid
Ⓓ identify

6 put on a pedestal
Ⓐ play
Ⓑ jacket
Ⓒ stand
Ⓓ record

7 a hidden defect
Ⓐ treasure
Ⓑ problem
Ⓒ result
Ⓓ room

8 true affection
Ⓐ caring
Ⓑ sickness
Ⓒ creation
Ⓓ story

9 missing pedal
Ⓐ flower part
Ⓑ foot control
Ⓒ diving platform
Ⓓ gym sock

10 broken manacle
Ⓐ handcuff
Ⓑ chair
Ⓒ fingernail
Ⓓ dream

Build New Words

Add Suffixes The suffixes *-ate*, *-inate*, and *-ize* can change a noun or an adjective to a verb. Add the suffixes to the vocabulary words below. Remove the letters indicated. Then add the suffix. Use the new word in a sentence.

Word	Subtract	Add	New Word	Sentence
germ		-inate		
immune	-e	-ize		
sanitary	-ary	-ize		
vaccine	-e	-ate		

Speak It! In your opinion, what is the future of medicine? Make a prediction about how doctors will treat sick or injured people in the future. Hold a debate or small-group discussion with your classmates. Use as many of the words on page 68 as you can.

Context Clues

for Word Wisdom

Wanted:

A Good Friend

What special things do you look for in a friend?
What makes someone want to be your friend?
Read this story about friendship. See if the same
things matter to you.

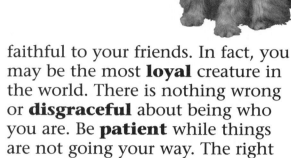

Behavior

**UNIT
4**

Dog sat whimpering next to a tree. "What's wrong?" Owl asked as he flew overhead. "Nobody likes me," **confessed** Dog. "Snake hisses at me every time he sees me. Squirrel won't share her food. Turtle complains that I'm noisy and that I rush around. I don't have any friends."

"We are all different," Owl replied. "It is important to find friends who like you for who you are. You have many fine traits. You may not be **cunning,** like Fox, but you don't try to trick people into doing what you want. You are **modest,** in contrast to Crow, who always boasts about his achievements. Unlike **stingy** Squirrel, who hides her nuts and won't share, you are **generous**. You share your affection with everyone. I'm glad you're different from **cranky** Snake, who hisses at everyone he sees. You, on the other hand, are rarely cross. You are always willing to be a friend to all.

"Never be **ashamed** of how you act," Owl continued. "You are so

faithful to your friends. In fact, you may be the most **loyal** creature in the world. There is nothing wrong or **disgraceful** about being who you are. Be **patient** while things are not going your way. The right friend will come along."

Dog began to feel a little prouder and more confident. Still, he was lonely.

One day, he was wandering near the edge of the forest when he saw two unusual animals. They walked on two paws instead of four and giggled as they tossed a round object back and forth. They were having so much fun that Dog could watch no longer. He raced after the ball and brought it back to the animals. They laughed and scratched him behind his ears. The three of them played together all afternoon.

That night when Dog saw Owl, Dog reported shyly, "I made two new friends today. Their names are Boy and Girl."

Context Clues Strategy

Look for What the Word Is Not Like

EXAMPLE: I would rather have a friend who is *sincere* than one who is fake or untrustworthy.

CLUE: The words *fake or untrustworthy* tell what the word *sincere* is unlike or contrasted with. Also, the words *rather...than* signal the clue.

Here are steps to figure out the meaning of the word *generous*, which appears in the story about Dog and his friends.

Read the sentence with the unknown word. Read some of the words around the unknown word.

Unlike stingy Squirrel, who hides her nuts and won't share, you are **generous**. *You share your affection with everyone.*

Look for context clues. What words that tell **What the Word Is Not Like** can you find?

Someone who is *generous* is not like someone who is *stingy* and *won't share*. The word *unlike* is also a clue.

Think about the context clues and other information you already know.

My teacher said I was *generous* because I share.

Predict a meaning for the word.

If someone is *generous*, he or she is willing to share.

Check the Word Wisdom Dictionary to be sure of the meaning.

Generous means "not selfish; willing to share."

Practice the Strategy Here is another boldfaced word from the story about Dog and his friends on page 72. Use the context clues strategy on page 73 to figure out the meaning of the word.

modest

📖 **Read** the sentence that uses the word *modest.* Read some of the sentences around the word *modest.*

🔍 **Look** for context clues. Can you find words that tell **What the Word Is Not Like?**

_____

_____

_____

💡 **Think** about the context clues. What other helpful information do you know?

_____

_____

_____

➡️ **Predict** a meaning for the word *modest.*

_____

_____

_____

✔️ **Check** your Word Wisdom Dictionary to be sure of the meaning of the word *modest.* Write the definition here.

_____

_____

_____

confess

cunning

✔modest

stingy

✔generous

cranky

ashamed

loyal

disgraceful

patient

Use Context Clues   The two vocabulary words that you have learned so far are checked off in the Word List. Write the other eight words from the Word List under "Vocabulary Word." Predict a meaning for each word under "Your Prediction." Then check the meanings in the Word Wisdom Dictionary. Write the definition that fits the context under "Dictionary Says."

	Vocabulary Word	Your Prediction	Dictionary Says
1			
2			
3			
4			
5			
6			
7			
8			

Process the Meanings

WORD LIST

- confess
- cunning
- modest
- stingy
- generous
- cranky
- ashamed
- loyal
- disgraceful
- patient

Use the Words Correctly in Writing Rewrite each sentence, using the word in parentheses.

1 Give as much as you can to support the team. (generous)

_____

2 The baby was upset when she became tired. (cranky)

_____

3 It's shameful to throw a lot of food away. (disgraceful)

_____

4 The sly dog sneaked into the dining room, which it knew was off limits. (cunning)

_____

5 My sister sticks up for me if someone teases me. (loyal)

_____

6 The selfish man refused to pay the worker the amount he had promised. (stingy)

_____

7 Never feel bad about yourself if you make a mistake; making mistakes is how we learn. (ashamed)

_____

8 Jim did not brag about his drawing talent. (modest)

_____

9 I have to admit that I don't like ice cream. (confess)

_____

10 It is hard to be willing to wait for your grades. (patient)

_____

Apply What You've Learned

Relate the Meanings   Use what you've learned to answer the questions.

1 Why might people **confess** to something they are **ashamed** of?

_____

_____

2 In your opinion, is it **disgraceful** to be **stingy**? Explain.

_____

_____

3 How could someone stay **patient** if he or she had to live with **cranky** people?

_____

_____

4 What would you think if someone **cunning** acted in a **modest** way?

_____

_____

5 Do you believe it is more important to be **generous** or to be **loyal**? Explain.

_____

_____

 Write It!   Write a paragraph about what you look for in a friend. Use as many words as you can from the Word List on page 76.

Latin and Greek Roots

for Word Wisdom

Muhammad Ali:
The Greatest

As a boxer, Muhammad Ali could "float like a butterfly and sting like a bee." As a man, he has inspired millions to stand up for their values.

Ali was born in 1942. He was named after his father, Cassius Clay Sr. Growing up in Louisville, Kentucky, Cassius Jr. was not a **genius**. In fact, he was a slow learner. A policeman urged him to train as a boxer. Cassius was **agreeable**. At age twelve, he began training. In high school, Cassius won 100 of 108 boxing matches. He won many championships, including two Golden Glove titles. At age eighteen, he won an Olympic gold medal.

Not a **passive** person, Cassius boasted about his fighting skills. His boasts were **genuine**. By age twenty-two, he was the heavyweight champion of the world. In the ring, Cassius was as **graceful** as he was strong. He threw powerful punches. Then he danced away from his opponent.

Cassius decided to join the Nation of Islam. Afterward, he changed his name to Muhammad Ali.

Ali does not like war. It is not **compatible** with his values. In 1967, he refused to serve in the Vietnam conflict. Many fans turned against him. He lost his boxing title. Ali was sentenced to prison, but his sentence was overturned.

Ali returned to the boxing ring in 1970. Over the years, he won and lost his title two more times. He fought his last fight in 1981. He lost, but he was nearly forty years old. Then his health started to fail. By 1982, Ali knew he had Parkinson's disease, a disease of the nervous system.

Ali no longer boxes. Still, he fights for what is right. Known as a **compassionate** person, he makes sure that young people learn job skills. **Grateful** for all he has, he helps victims of war. Now more **genteel** than fierce, Ali helps children around the world.

Ali is **gracious** to his fans. He is still one of the best-known people in the world. In 1996, millions watched him light the Olympic torch in Atlanta.

Muhammad Ali will always be admired for his strength, in and out of the ring.

Practice the Context Clues Strategy Here is one of the boldfaced words from the essay on page 78. Use the context clues strategy you learned in Part 1 on page 73 to figure out the meaning of this word.

genteel

Read the sentence that uses the word *genteel* and some of the sentences around it.

Look for context clues to the word's meaning. Can you find words that tell **What the Word Is Not Like?**

_____

_____

_____

Think about the context clues and other information you may already know.

_____

_____

_____

Predict a meaning for the word *genteel*.

_____

_____

_____

Check your Word Wisdom Dictionary to be sure of the meaning of the word *genteel*. Write the definition here.

_____

_____

_____

🔒 Unlock the Meanings

Many words you use are made from Latin or Greek roots. Knowing the meanings of different roots can often help you figure out the meanings of new words. The following roots relate to behavior.

Latin Root: **pass, pat**

meaning: to bear or suffer

English word: *patient*

meaning: able to wait; willing to put up with problems

Latin and Greek Root: **gen**

meaning: to produce; a kind of

English word: *generous*

meaning: not selfish; willing to share

Latin Root: **grac, grat**

meaning: thankful

English word: *gracious*

meaning: showing kindness, courtesy, or tact

WORD LIST

- genius
- agreeable
- passive
- genuine
- graceful
- compatible
- compassionate
- grateful
- genteel
- gracious

Sort by Roots Find these roots in the Word List. Write each word on a line below the correct root. One word does not have the root *grat* or *grac*, but it comes from those roots. Write that word on the line with the other *grat* and *grac* words. Then think of other words you know that come from the same Latin or Greek roots.

Latin Root: grac, grat	Latin and Greek Root: gen	Latin Root: pass, pat
_____	_____	_____
_____	_____	_____
_____	_____	_____
_____	_____	_____
_____	_____	_____

Behavior

Prefix	Meaning
com-	together, with

Example

com- (with) + pat (bear) + -ible (able)
= compatible

Use Roots and Prefixes Circle any roots and prefixes you find in the boldfaced words below. Use context clues, roots, and prefixes to write the meaning of each word. Then check your definition in the Word Wisdom Dictionary.

1 Even someone as brilliant as a **genius** must do his or her homework.

_____

2 The **graceful** ballet dancer was a pleasure to watch.

_____

3 My brother is more **genteel** since he took a class in good manners.

_____

4 She was **agreeable** to our plan to go swimming.

_____

5 We felt very welcomed by the **gracious** host.

_____

6 A person is **compassionate** if he wants to help others who are suffering.

_____

7 If something is not fake, then it is **genuine**.

_____

8 If you appreciate what others do for you, you are **grateful**.

_____

9 Well-matched roommates are **compatible**.

_____

10 People who are **passive** do not take charge of their life.

_____

Process the Meanings

WORD LIST

genius
agreeable
passive
genuine
graceful
compatible
compassionate
grateful
genteel
gracious

Choose the Correct Word Here is an example of a letter written a long time ago. Write the word from the Word List that best completes each sentence.

August 5, 1912

Dear Aunt Harriet,

I speak only the truth when I say that it was a real,

1 _____ pleasure to visit you last week.

I am very **2** _____ for my time at the

seashore. If it is **3** _____ to you, I would

like to return next summer. Cousin Louise and I are so

4 _____. She has the most kind and

5 _____ manners! I can't imagine visiting

more **6** _____ people. The journey home

passed quickly. We traveled by a pond with a pair of

7 _____ swans. One of the birds was

injured, so our kind and **8** _____ driver

stopped to rescue it. The bird was surprisingly quite

9 _____ as the driver removed some wire

from its beak. We said the driver was remarkable; a

10 _____ for figuring out how to do it

without upsetting the bird! Thank you for a lovely visit.

Most sincerely yours,

Your niece Emily

Apply What You've Learned

Find the Examples Write **E** next to each sentence only if it is an example of the boldfaced word.

1 **compatible** You like being with a friend because you have

similar interests. _____

2 **gracious** Your cousin is a great dancer. _____

3 **genteel** You shake hands when introduced. _____

4 **genius** The employee came up with a new invention. _____

Demonstrate Word Knowledge Follow the directions below.

5 Describe a time when you acted in a **compassionate** way.

_____

6 Describe how an animal might act in a way that is **passive**.

_____

7 Describe a time when you wondered if something was **genuine**.

_____

8 Describe a time when you were **grateful** for something.

_____

9 Describe something you once saw that was very **graceful**.

_____

10 Tell whether you'd be **agreeable** to six hours of homework.

_____

Speak It! Tell about a person you would like to know better. Use as many words as you can from the Word List on page 82.

Reference Skills

Wild Behavior:
Gorilla Watch

What are gorillas like? Do they really act like people? Can we find out before they disappear from Earth?

People have always been **curious** about gorillas. However, much of the African forest where gorillas live is gone. It has been turned into towns, villages, and camps for logging and mining. The number of gorillas living in the wild drops each year. Some kinds of gorillas are endangered. It's getting harder to find gorillas to study. Still, people are trying to protect them. In 1993, a park was created in the Congo. It includes a large, swampy clearing. The clearing covers about twenty-five acres and was probably created by elephants. This clearing attracts many animals. There, scientists can observe wild gorillas.

We once thought that gorillas avoid water. Not **hesitant** about getting wet, these gorillas jump right into the water. They like to sit in it and munch on nearby plants. Gorillas live in groups. A large male leads each group. The group includes young males, females, and babies. Groups often eat side by side. Mostly, they are **courteous** to each other.

Still, a group leader may feel **anxious** if another large male gets too close. The leader might slap the water with his huge hand. The sharp noise is often enough to scare away the **inconsiderate** male. Sometimes the leader also soaks the offender with a large spray of water.

An **adventurous** young male sometimes tries to lure away females from other groups. He might try to scare the females into following him. The young male might shriek at them loudly. He might beat his chest to show his **ferocious** power. The older male may watch him for a while. Often he will ignore him. If he feels threatened, he may become **furious**. Then he will charge the younger gorilla. This quickly puts a stop to his **disrespectful** actions. The intruder, now **humble,** runs for his life.

Watching gorillas allows scientists to better understand them. We need to learn as much as we can about these animals. Then we will be better able to protect them. We don't want them to disappear from Earth. Learning about animals and their needs also helps us learn about ourselves.

Practice the Context Clues Strategy Here is one of the boldfaced words from the essay on page 84. Use the context clues strategy you learned in Part 1 on page 73 to figure out the meaning of this word.

hesitant

Read the sentence that uses the word *hesitant* and some of the sentences around it.

Look for context clues to the word's meaning. Can you find words that tell **What the Word Is Not Like?**

_____

_____

_____

Think about the context clues and other information you may already know.

_____

_____

_____

Predict a meaning for the word *hesitant*.

_____

_____

_____

Check your Word Wisdom Dictionary to be sure of the meaning of the word *hesitant*. Write the definition here.

_____

_____

_____

Unlock the Meanings

Dictionary Definitions: Multiple Meanings

Some words have more than one meaning. Multiple meanings are usually listed in a separate dictionary entry. The entries are marked with a raised number. Dictionaries also use abbreviations to refer to the part of speech of the word. For example, *n.* stands for noun, *v.* stands for verb, and *adj.* stands for adjective.

When you are looking for the meaning of an unfamiliar word, think about the context in which the word appears. Choose the definition that fits the context in which the unfamiliar word is used. Here are two dictionary entries that give multiple meanings for the word *anxious*.

> **anx•ious**[1] /ăngk′ shəs/ *adj.* worried; uneasy. *We became anxious when our dog didn't return immediately.*
>
> **anx•ious**[2] /ăngk′ shəs/ *adj.* eagerly wishing. *They were anxious for the party to begin.*

Choose the Dictionary Definition   Using the dictionary entries above, choose the correct definition for the word *anxious* in each sentence below. Write the number of the definition on the blank line.

1 Mr. and Mrs. Ruiz are anxious to meet us. _____

2 Everyone is anxious for summer vacation to begin. _____

3 Don't be anxious about taking the test; you will pass

easily. _____

4 We are anxious to celebrate your birthday. _____

5 My cats become anxious during thunderstorms. _____

Find the Meaning
1. Use context clues.
2. Look for a familiar root, prefix, or suffix.
3. If the context or a word part doesn't help, check the dictionary.

Define the Words Follow the steps above to write the meaning of each boldfaced word. Write 1, 2, or 3 to show the steps you used.

WORD LIST

curious
hesitant
courteous
anxious
inconsiderate
adventurous
ferocious
furious
disrespectful
humble

1 **Adventurous** people would enjoy rafting on high waves.

_____

2 It is **disrespectful** to talk during a violin performance.

_____

3 **Humble** people do not brag about what they do well.

_____

4 Are you **curious** about what life will be like in the future?

_____

5 The mother bear became **ferocious** when her cub was in danger.

_____

6 I'd be **furious** if someone tried to hurt my little brother.

_____

7 The shy little boy was **hesitant** about petting the big dog.

_____

8 Keeping other people waiting is **inconsiderate**.

_____

9 It is **courteous** to respond when someone asks you a question.

_____

10 The man looked **anxious** as he crossed the rising stream.

_____

Process the Meanings

WORD LIST

- curious
- hesitant
- courteous
- anxious
- inconsiderate
- adventurous
- ferocious
- furious
- disrespectful
- humble

Build Word Ladders Use the words in the box below to make a word ladder. Order the lists with the most positive characteristic at the top and the most negative characteristic at the bottom.

> disrespectful   courteous   inconsiderate

1 _____

2 _____

3 _____

> curious   hesitant   adventurous

4 _____

5 _____

6 _____

Match the Meanings Match each vocabulary word with its correct definition.

Vocabulary Word	Definition
7 _____ anxious	a. wild and fierce
8 _____ humble	b. meek or modest
9 _____ furious	c. extremely angry
10 _____ ferocious	d. worried or nervous

Apply What You've Learned

Complete the Sentences   Write an ending for each sentence.

1 Something that you are **curious** about is _____

_____

2 One way people could be **courteous** is _____

_____

3 Something that makes many students **anxious** is _____

_____

4 If you are **adventurous**, you might enjoy _____

_____

5 Something that is **inconsiderate** to do is _____

_____

Demonstrate Word Knowledge   Answer the questions.

6 How could a storm and an animal both be **ferocious**?

_____

7 Would you be **hesitant** to hold a harmless snake? Explain.

_____

8 What might make a person **furious**? _____

9 What might a **disrespectful** person do? _____

10 Would you describe yourself as **humble**? Explain.

_____

Write It! Write a description of your personality.
Use words from the Word List on page 88.

Review

for Word Wisdom

WORD LIST

- confess
- cunning
- modest
- stingy
- generous
- cranky
- ashamed
- loyal
- disgraceful
- patient
- genius
- agreeable
- passive
- genuine
- graceful
- compatible
- compassionate
- grateful
- genteel
- gracious
- curious
- hesitant
- courteous
- anxious
- inconsiderate
- adventurous
- ferocious
- furious
- disrespectful
- humble

Sort by Connotation Read the words in the Word List. Pick the words that could describe someone in a positive way. Then choose the words that could describe someone in a negative way. Circle any words with the roots *pass* or *pat*, *grac* or *grat*, and *gen*.

Positive 👍   👎 **Negative**

Find Related Words Read the sentences below. Look at the underlined word part. Write the vocabulary word that contains the underlined word part and fits the context.

1 I'd be _____ if you would <u>grate</u> the

cheese.

2 Karen has a polite, <u>gentle</u> nature. Her manners are quite

_____.

3 Tom was so <u>gen</u>erous in his praise, I wondered if he was

_____.

4 Littering their neighbors' yard was dis<u>grace</u>ful after the

neighbors had been so _____ to them.

5 Alex is very _____ on the tennis <u>court</u>.

He never yells or throws his racquet.

6 I _____ that I can't <u>con</u>trol my dog.

7 The man is a _____, and he is kind

and <u>gen</u>tle because his inventions helped others.

8 When Lola saw how <u>pat</u>ient Tia was, she knew they

would be _____ team members.

9 The dancer was very <u>grac</u>ious when we told her how

_____ her dance performance was.

10 More people brag about themselves in <u>mod</u>ern times

compared with long ago. They are not as

_____ as people were in the past.

Taking Vocabulary Tests

TEST-TAKING STRATEGY

Read the directions carefully when you take a vocabulary test. If the directions tell you to find the OPPOSITE, or ANTONYM, don't get tricked by answer choices that are synonyms or near synonyms. This test asks you to find the word that has the OPPOSITE meaning of the underlined word.

Sample:

passive person
- (A) quiet
- (B) sleepy
- (C) athletic
- (D) active

Practice Test Circle the letter of the answer choice that means the OPPOSITE of the underlined vocabulary word.

1 seem <u>furious</u>
- (A) tired
- (B) angry
- (C) pleased
- (D) upset

2 feel <u>ashamed</u>
- (A) foolish
- (B) proud
- (C) hungry
- (D) moved

3 <u>ferocious</u> animal
- (A) tame
- (B) wild
- (C) four-legged
- (D) sure-footed

4 <u>cranky</u> child
- (A) tired
- (B) grouchy
- (C) agreeable
- (D) quiet

5 <u>inconsiderate</u> act
- (A) short
- (B) careful
- (C) careless
- (D) thoughtful

6 <u>curious</u> look
- (A) funny
- (B) bored
- (C) energetic
- (D) puzzled

7 <u>disrespectful</u> tone
- (A) loud
- (B) rude
- (C) hurtful
- (D) polite

8 <u>anxious</u> moment
- (A) calm
- (B) quiet
- (C) weepy
- (D) cheerful

9 <u>agreeable</u> person
- (A) willing
- (B) honest
- (C) unwilling
- (D) happy

10 <u>hesitant</u> step
- (A) running
- (B) small
- (C) timid
- (D) bold

Play with Language

King Arthur's Code According to legend, the Knights of the Round Table who served King Arthur were expected to follow a strict code of conduct. Check the Word List on page 90 to find synonyms for the characteristics below. Then unscramble the circled letters to find the name of the knights' code.

Traits of Knights of the Round Table

1 daring: __ __ ◯ __ __ __ __ __ __ __

2 polite: ◯ __ __ __ __ __ __ __ __

3 modest: ◯ __ __ __ ◯ __

4 faithful: __ __ ◯◯ __

5 caring about someone's suffering:

__ __ __ __ __ __ __ ◯ __ __ __ __ __

6 unselfish: __ __ __ __ ◯ __ __ __

Code of __ __ __ __ __ __ __ __

Speak It! Suppose you were to start a club whose members did good deeds in secret. How would you choose the club members? What kinds of deeds would the club members do? Use as many words as you can from the Word List on page 90.

Context Clues

for Word Wisdom

Step by Step:

Erik Weihenmayer

Small challenges keep some people from following their dreams. Other people who are challenged in large ways manage to make their dreams come true. Read about climber Erik Weihenmayer, who faces very large challenges and manages to make very large dreams come true.

Movement

UNIT 5

Far away in Nepal lie the world's tallest mountains, the Himalayas. You may think that these peaks are **impassable** to all but the world's fittest climbers. This is generally true. However, the jagged peaks do not stop climber Erik Weihenmayer, who is blind.

Erik has never let blindness be a **barrier** to things he wants to do. He pushes himself to try things that sighted people may not be willing to try. Erik says he might never have climbed Mount Everest if he hadn't lost his sight.

At nearly thirty thousand feet high, Mount Everest is the highest mountain in the world. Like the dangers in any steep, snowy place, its **hazards** include strong winds and severe cold. Climbers must be careful of avalanches. Deep, narrow canyons in the ice are another hidden danger.

Like the rate of speed of any other mountain climber, Erik's **pace** up Mount Everest is slow. He follows the sound of a bell that his climbing buddies carry. He uses long poles for balance as he **treks** up the trail.

Local Sherpa guides **accompany** Himalayan climbers. They are a crucial part of any **expedition** in these mountains. Sherpas act as **porters**. They often carry the climbers' heavy packs up Everest. Erik, however, carries his own pack.

Whenever he climbs, Erik can hear what he calls open and closed spaces. He listens for a drop-off into space. Sounds also tell him when he reaches some type of barrier. He is surprisingly **mobile**. Wherever he goes, he keeps up with the rest of his team. He tackles the most **grueling** and difficult climbs the world has to offer. In fact, Erik Weihenmayer is the first blind person to reach the top of the highest mountains on all seven of the world's continents.

Context Clues Strategy

Look for What the Word Is Like

EXAMPLE: A *gorge*, like any narrow, rocky path, is a danger for climbers.

CLUE: The words *like any narrow, rocky path* tell you what a *gorge* is like.

Here are the steps for using this context clues strategy to figure out the meaning of the word *pace* from the article on page 94.

Read the sentence with the unknown word and some of the sentences around it.

* * * * *

Like the rate of speed of any other mountain climber, Erik's **pace** *up Mount Everest is slow.*

Look for context clues. What words that tell **What the Word Is Like** can you find?

* * * * *

The sentence says that Erik's *pace* is like *the rate of speed* of other climbers.

Think about the context clues and other helpful information you know.

* * * * *

My track coach tells us to pick up the pace when we run. She means for us to run faster.

Predict a meaning for the word *pace*.

* * * * *

Pace could be someone's speed of moving.

Check the Word Wisdom Dictionary to be sure of the meaning.

* * * * *

Pace means "the rate of speed of walking or running."

Unlock the Meanings

Practice the Strategy Here is one of the boldfaced words from the article on page 94. Use the context clues strategy on page 95 to figure out the meaning of the word.

---

hazards

📖 **Read** the sentence that uses the word *hazards* and some of the sentences around it.

🔍 **Look** for context clues. What words that tell **What the Word Is Like** can you find?

_____

_____

_____

💡 **Think** about the context clues. What other helpful information do you know?

_____

_____

_____

➡️ **Predict** a meaning for the word *hazards*.

_____

_____

_____

✔️ **Check** your Word Wisdom Dictionary to be sure of the meaning of the word *hazard*. Which of the meanings for the word *hazard* fits the context?

_____

_____

Use Context Clues You have been introduced to two vocabulary words from the article on page 94. Those words are checked off in the Word List. Under "Vocabulary Word" below, write the other eight words from the Word List. Use context clues to predict a meaning for each word under "Your Prediction." Then look up the meanings in the Word Wisdom Dictionary. Write the definition under "Dictionary Says."

WORD LIST

impassable

barrier

✔ hazard

✔ pace

trek

accompany

expedition

porter

mobile

grueling

	Vocabulary Word	Your Prediction	Dictionary Says
1			
2			
3			
4			
5			
6			
7			
8			

WORD LIST

impassable
barrier
hazard
pace
trek
accompany
expedition
porter
mobile
grueling

Match the Definitions Write the word from the Word List that matches each definition.

1 hike   _____

2 danger   _____

3 movable   _____

4 not able to be crossed   _____

5 something that blocks the way _____

Choose the Correct Word Write the word from the Word List that best completes each sentence in this friendly letter. Do not repeat any of the words from the exercise above.

Dear Neil,

    Our scout troop hiked in the mountains last weekend. My

mom decided that she wanted to hike, too, and that she

would **6** _____ us. We walked at a quick

7 _____ for five hours. We all found the

hike tough and **8** _____. Mom's back

was sore from carrying a heavy pack. When we got home,

Mom told Dad he should plan to go on our next

9 _____. She said he could be her

10 _____!

                                        Your friend,

                                        Marcus

Apply What You've Learned

Relate the Meanings Answer the questions. Use the boldfaced words in your answers.

1 What kinds of **hazards** might slow a hiker's **pace**?

_____

_____

2 What kind of **barriers** could make a road **impassable**?

_____

_____

3 Why must a **porter** be **mobile**?

_____

_____

4 If you were to **trek** across the United States, would you find it **grueling**? Why or why not?

_____

_____

_____

5 Would you like to **accompany** people on an **expedition** to the North Pole? Why or why not?

_____

_____

_____

 Write It! Describe a hike you once took. Use as many words from the Word List in Part 1 as you can.

PART 2 Latin Roots
for Word Wisdom

East Meets West:
Crossing the Country by Rail

Traveling was not easy in the early 1800s. There were no cars or airplanes. Goods were moved on ships, not trucks.

In the early 1800s the main means of **locomotion** were by foot, on horseback, or in a covered wagon. Many people rode trains, but they went no farther west than the Mississippi River. It was difficult to **transport** goods beyond this river. The government wanted to **promote** travel to the West. In 1862, Congress decided to **expand** the railroads, just like it was building more roads. The rails would stretch across the nation to link both coasts.

Two companies built the first railway to cross the country. One started in Omaha, Nebraska, laying tracks toward the West. The other company started in Sacramento, California, laying tracks toward the East. The tracks would finally meet in Utah.

The California crew began in 1863. At first, laying track was easy. Then the crew reached the Sierra Nevada Mountains. There was no **passage** through the mountains.

Hills had to be leveled. Valleys had to be filled in. At one place, workers had to drill through solid rock that stretched for a quarter of a mile! Blasting a tunnel through this rock took a whole year.

The Nebraska crew began in 1865. They faced bad weather across the Plains. They also faced angry Native Americans who did not want the railroad crews to **trespass** on their land.

Laying the track took years. The two companies raced each other. Each wanted to **surpass** the other one. Finally, crews from both companies could see each other. The tracks met at Promontory Point, Utah. The date was May 10, 1869. The two companies had laid two thousand miles of track.

At last, people could ride a train from the East Coast to the West Coast. Now people in the East could **import** fruit from the West. Eastern states could **export** steel and other products to the West. Trains began carrying **portable** goods across the nation.

Although fewer people ride them now, trains played a major role in the settling of the West. And they still transport needed goods today.

Practice the Context Clues Strategy Here is one of the boldfaced words from the essay on page 100. Use the context clues strategy you learned in Part 1 on page 95 to figure out the meaning of this word.

expand

Read the sentence that uses the word *expand* and some of the sentences around it.

Look for context clues to the word's meaning. What words can you find that tell **What the Word Is Like?**

_____

_____

_____

Think about the context clues and other information you may already know.

_____

_____

_____

Predict a meaning for the word *expand*.

_____

_____

_____

Check your Word Wisdom Dictionary to be sure of the meaning of the word *expand*. Write the definition here.

_____

_____

_____

Unlock the Meanings

Many words you use come from Latin roots. Knowing the meaning of different roots will help you figure out the meaning of new words. Several words you learned in Part 1 have a Latin root. Each root on this page relates to movement.

Latin Root: **port**
meaning: to carry
English word: *porter*
meaning: person who carries

Latin Root: **pan, pass**
meaning: to spread, to step
English word: *impassable*
meaning: not able to be crossed over or passed

Latin Root: **mot, mov**
meaning: to move
English word: *mobile*
meaning: able to move

WORD LIST

locomotion
transport
promote
expand
passage
trespass
surpass
import
export
portable

Sort by Roots Find these roots in the Word List. Write each word on a line under the correct root. Then think of other words that come from the same Latin roots. Write each word in the correct place.

Movement

Latin Root: port

Latin Root: pan, pass

Latin Root: mot, mov

Prefix	Meaning
im-	in, not
sur-	over, above

Example

sur- (over) + pass (step) = surpass

Use Roots and Prefixes Circle any roots and prefixes that you find in the boldfaced words. Use context clues, roots, and prefixes to write the meaning of each word. Check your definitions in a dictionary.

1 Eating too many desserts will **expand** a person's waistline.

_____

2 Companies **promote** new bands by playing their music on the radio.

_____

3 Pipelines **transport** gas from one part of the country to another.

_____

4 This birthday will **surpass** everything you ever hoped it would be.

_____

5 My favorite kind of **locomotion** is a train ride.

_____

6 Doesn't his family **import** spices from around the world?

_____

7 Can you walk through that small **passage** between the rocks?

_____

8 What products does the United States **export** to other countries?

_____

9 My grandfather carries a **portable** chair when he goes to a museum.

_____

10 They don't like it when people **trespass** on their property.

_____

WORD LIST

locomotion

transport

promote

expand

passage

trespass

surpass

import

export

portable

Replace the Words   Write the word from the Word List that means nearly the same as the underlined word or words in each sentence.

_____ **1** Reading books will <u>increase the size or number of</u> the ideas in your mind.

_____ **2** Did you <u>do better than</u> your score on the last spelling test?

_____ **3** Is that box <u>easy to carry</u>?

_____ **4** Does Italy <u>sell</u> many pairs of shoes <u>to the United States</u>?

_____ **5** The sign warned people not to <u>go onto private property</u>.

Choose the Correct Words Write the word from the Word List that best completes each sentence.

6 We had a special science fair to _____ ways to prevent pollution.

7 They heard voices in the narrow _____ between the buildings.

8 Skipping and running are both forms of

_____.

9 Some factories _____ raw materials from other countries to make new products.

10 Seeing that movie will _____ you to another time.

Apply What You've Learned

Complete the Sentences Complete each sentence below.

1 Children might **trespass** if _____

_____

2 Two forms of **locomotion** are _____

_____

3 An idea that the government might **promote** is _____

_____

4 I **surpassed** what I thought I could do when I _____

_____

5 Something I own that is **portable** is _____

6 A plane is likely to **transport** _____

7 Two things that can **expand** are _____

_____

8 Some things that the United States **imports** are _____

_____

9 A narrow **passage** that I once went through was _____

_____

10 A product that Europe **exports** to the United States is

_____

Speak It! Tell what you would take if you were moving to a new place. How would you carry these items? Use as many words from the Word List in Part 2 as you can.

Reference Skills

How to Ride a Horse

Many children want to have a horse, but few get their wish. If you get a chance to ride a horse, the tips in this essay will help you enjoy the experience.

To mount a horse, move to its left side. Make sure the strap holding the saddle on (the girth) is tight. A loose girth will allow the saddle to slip from side to side or to **migrate** along the horse's back. To get on the horse, step up on a mounting block to **elevate** your body and make mounting easier. Hold the reins in your left hand. Put that hand on the raised front part (the pommel) of the saddle. Hold the reins firmly so the horse does not **shuffle** around as you try to mount. However, do not pull back on the reins, as that will cause the horse to **retreat**.

Put your left foot in the ring that supports the rider's foot (the stirrup) and your right hand on the back of the saddle. Then jump up and swing your right leg over the horse, moving your right hand as your leg goes by.

Be careful not to kick the horse, or it may move forward. If you

accidentally kick the horse hard, it may even **bolt** and run away. After that, the horse may try to **evade** you, like any animal tries to get away from something scary.

To ask the horse to walk, squeeze its sides gently with your lower legs. After it starts to **advance,** relax your legs. Some horses need a gentle kick with both heels before they will move forward.

A trot is a slow run. To ask the horse to trot, squeeze its sides with your legs again, applying more pressure this time. A **canter** is a faster run. After your horse is trotting, squeeze your legs again to ask it to canter.

To get the horse to turn or **rotate,** gently pull back on one rein while using your legs to encourage the horse to go forward. To stop the horse, gently pull back on both reins and squeeze with your legs again. If the horse is running, encourage it to move from a canter, to a trot, to a walk, and then to a halt.

Now you are ready to ride! If you **conduct** yourself with confidence around the horse, it will feel more relaxed, and you both will enjoy the ride.

Practice the Context Clues Strategy Here is one of the boldfaced words from the riding instructions on page 106. Use the context clues strategy you learned in Part 1 on page 95 to figure out the meaning of this word.

evade

📖 **Read** the sentence that uses the word *evade* and some of the sentences around it.

🔍 **Look** for context clues to the word's meaning. What words can you find that tell **What the Word Is Like?**

_____

_____

_____

💡 **Think** about the context clues and other information you may already know.

_____

_____

_____

➡ **Predict** a meaning for the word *evade*.

_____

_____

_____

✔ **Check** your Word Wisdom Dictionary to be sure of the meaning of the word *evade*. Write the definition here.

_____

_____

_____

Unlock the Meanings

Computer Thesaurus A thesaurus is a reference tool that is useful when you are looking for just the right word. It lists words that are synonyms (words that have the same or almost the same meaning).

If you use a computer program for writing, it probably has a built-in thesaurus. To use a **computer thesaurus,** click on the word for which you need a synonym. Then go to the "Tools" menu and open the thesaurus. A list of synonyms will be displayed.

Here are some synonyms that a computer thesaurus might give for the word *advance.*

go forward	bring forward	march
set forward	push forward	

Choose the Synonyms Write the synonym from the box above that best replaces the word *advance* in each sentence.

1 Don't forget to *advance* your watch when you enter the new

time zone. _____

2 You can *advance* a pawn two spaces in its first chess move.

_____

3 The hikers can *advance* easily to the next hill and wait for us

there. _____

4 When will the parade of drummers *advance* to Park Square?

_____

5 Those students who want to *advance* the idea of a school

appreciation day are themselves appreciated!

_____

Find the Meaning
1. Use context clues.
2. Look for a familiar root, prefix, or suffix.
3. If the context or a word part doesn't help, check the dictionary.

Define the Words Follow the steps above to write the meaning of each boldfaced word. Write 1, 2, or 3 to show the steps you used.

WORD LIST

migrate

elevate

shuffle

retreat

bolt

evade

advance

canter

rotate

conduct

1 Gray whales **migrate** between California and Mexico.

_____

2 The horse **cantered**, moving between a walk and a gallop.

_____

3 It's so cold that I must **retreat** indoors.

_____

4 Do not **shuffle** your feet along the new wood floors.

_____

5 Our winning team will **advance** to the finals.

_____

6 When I started the drill, the cat **bolted** for the door.

_____

7 Please **conduct** yourself properly when our visitors are here.

_____

8 **Elevate** the child so that he can reach the table.

_____

9 The spy tried to **evade** being caught.

_____

10 The earth **rotates** on its axis each day.

_____

WORD LIST

- migrate
- elevate
- shuffle
- retreat
- bolt
- evade
- advance
- canter
- rotate
- conduct

Complete the Groups Choose the best vocabulary word to go in each group.

1 dash   rush   _____

2 cycle   spin   _____

3 trot   gallop   _____

4 lift   raise   _____

5 drag feet   slide   _____

6 commute   travel   _____

Complete the Paragraph Choose the vocabulary word that best completes each sentence in the paragraph. Do not repeat any of the words that you used above.

The Continental soldier hid behind a tree as he tried to

7 _____ enemy bullets. The Redcoats

continued their **8** _____ across the field.

Even though the Americans were outnumbered, they would

not **9** _____. They would always

10 _____ themselves with bravery and

pride throughout the war.

Apply What You've Learned

Demonstrate Word Knowledge   Answer the questions.

1 Why would you want to **advance** in school?

_____

2 What might make a young child **bolt**?

_____

3 In which place would you be willing to **conduct** a tour? Why?

_____

4 What would make you want to **retreat**?

_____

5 What would happen to you if you **rotated** quickly five times?

_____

6 Would you ever want to **migrate**? Why or why not?

_____

7 Which animals would never **canter**? Why?

_____

8 In a large store, what could **elevate** people or merchandise?

_____

9 How could you **evade** a bad storm?

_____

10 When is someone likely to **shuffle** his or her feet?

_____

Write It!   Suppose you discovered a secret passage and decided to follow it. Write about what happened and where you went. Use as many words from the Word List in Part 3 as you can.

Review

for Word Wisdom

WORD LIST

impassable
barrier
hazard
pace
trek
accompany
expedition
porter
mobile
grueling
locomotion
transport
promote
expand
passage
trespass
surpass
import
export
portable
migrate
elevate
shuffle
retreat
bolt
evade
advance
canter
rotate
conduct

Sort by Syllables Say each word to yourself. Count the syllables. Then write the word in the correct column. Cross the words off the list as you work. When you are finished, circle every word that has the root *port, pan, pass,* or *mot.*

One Syllable	Two Syllables	Three Syllables	Four Syllables

Choose the Best Words Decide which vocabulary word could best replace the boldfaced word or words in each sentence. Write the letter of your choice on the line.

____ **1** A switch allowed the patient to **raise** the head or foot of her bed.
a. expand   b. export   c. elevate   d. shuffle

____ **2** To keep automobiles off the beach, the town put up **some things that block the way.**
a. hazards   b. porters   c. passages   d. barriers

____ **3** The heat made chopping firewood **difficult** work.
a. grueling   b. portable   c. mobile   d. impassable

____ **4** To keep from slipping on the wet floor, we held onto the handrail as we **dragged our feet** down the hall.
a. bolted   b. retreated   c. shuffled   d. cantered

____ **5** My friend agreed to **go with** me to the mall.
a. transport   b. accompany   c. promote   d. import

____ **6** Thomas Jefferson approved the **trip of discovery** through the unknown areas of the Northwest.
a. advance   b. expedition   c. retreat   d. pace

____ **7** The floodwaters made many of the roads **impossible to travel across.**
a. portable   b. grueling   c. mobile   d. impassable

____ **8** After dinner, we **went back** to the living room and continued watching the football game on TV.
a. surpassed   b. shuffled   c. retreated   d. advanced

____ **9** It is important to dress properly to **take a long difficult journey** in the mountains.
a. trek   b. promote   c. canter   d. rotate

____ **10** The bird watchers **moved forward** slowly through the forest so that they would not frighten away the rare woodpecker.
a. elevated   b. exported   c. advanced   d. transported

Taking Vocabulary Tests

When you take a vocabulary test, be sure you understand what the directions ask you to do. Some vocabulary tests use analogies. Think about how the two words in the first part of the analogy are related. Then decide which words in the other part are related in the same way. Don't be tricked by words that make sense but do not show the same relationship.

Sample:

Drop is to lower as **elevate** is to ____.
(A) find
(B) trap
(C) sink
(D) raise

Practice Test Fill in the letter of the answer choice that correctly completes the analogy.

1 Climb is to ladder as **rotate** is to ____.
(A) car
(B) ski
(C) swimming pool
(D) merry-go-round

2 Speed is to road as **pace** is to ____.
(A) snail
(B) hiker
(C) trail
(D) pack

3 Bird is to **migrate** as person is to ____.
(A) travel
(B) glasses
(C) plane
(D) boat

4 Danger is to fire as **hazard** is to ____.
(A) food
(B) kitten
(C) ice
(D) laugh

5 Crawl is to slow as **bolt** is to ____.
(A) run
(B) fast
(C) horse
(D) lightning

6 Fun is to party as **grueling** is to ____.
(A) hard
(B) easy
(C) work
(D) play

7 Continue is to go ahead as **retreat** is to ____.
(A) go faster
(B) go back
(C) turn off
(D) look back

8 Bark is to dog as **canter** is to ____.
(A) fish
(B) horse
(C) turtle
(D) bird

9 Doorway is to enter as **barrier** is to ____.
(A) block
(B) invite
(C) pay
(D) hurry

10 Seek is to friend as **evade** is to ____.
(A) jungle
(B) kitten
(C) country
(D) enemy

Build New Words

Use Suffixes to Change Verbs to Nouns

The suffixes *-ion* and *-ation* mean "the act of" and change a verb to a noun. Complete the chart. Check the spellings and meanings in a dictionary.

Verb	Noun with -ion or -ation	Meaning
1 rotate		
2 transport		
3 migrate		
4 elevate		
5 promote		

Write a sentence using each noun from the chart.

6 _____

_____

7 _____

_____

8 _____

_____

9 _____

_____

10 _____

_____

Speak It! Tell about a barrier you once overcame and how you did it. Use several vocabulary words from this unit.

Context Clues

for Word Wisdom

Christo and Jeanne-Claude: Environmental Artists

If you think art is something you see only in museums, you'll soon change your mind. Read this article about Christo and Jeanne-Claude, creators of art in the environment.

Christo and Jeanne-Claude, Wrapped Trees, Fondation Beyeler and Berower Park, Riehen, Switzerland. 1997-98.

Look quickly if you want to see the work of artists Christo and Jeanne-Claude. This married couple has created art together for more than forty years. Their sculptures aren't **permanent**. In fact, after years of planning, their works may last only a few weeks.

Christo and Jeanne-Claude use **fabric,** or cloth, as a form of art. The flat, **formless** fabric has no shape. It takes on the **dimensions** —the height, width, and length— of the object it wraps.

Some art is realistic and shows a person or an object that you can recognize. Some art is **abstract.** The art of Christo and Jeanne-Claude is environmental. Its beauty lies in how it fits into the world around it.

These artists use **synthetic** cloth, not natural fabric, to create amazing effects. Wrapped trees look like huge lollipops with **irregular** edges, rather than smooth, even ones. Wrapped rocks along a coast **shimmer,** gently shining with sea spray.

One of their best known works is called *Running Fence*. They hung 24½ miles of white fabric on more than 2,000 steel poles across northern California. Miles of cloth **billowed** in the wind. In contrast to cloth that is not lit by any light source, the fluttering fabric was **luminous** as it reflected the sunlight. The project took almost four years to finish, but removal began two weeks after it was done.

Christo and Jeanne-Claude don't sell their projects. They sell drawings of their art and early works, instead. They pay for their projects with their own money. When a display is taken down, the art site is returned to its natural state and the materials are recycled.

Context Clues Strategy

Look for Words That Mean the Opposite

EXAMPLE: Lines that are *horizontal*, rather than lines that run top to bottom, have been shown to have a calming effect.

CLUE: The words *rather than* give a clue. Lines that run *top to bottom* are the opposite of *horizontal* lines. Horizontal lines go across, from one side to another.

Here is another strategy for using context clues to understand the meaning of the word *irregular* from the article on page 116.

Read the sentence with the unknown word and some of the sentences around it.

*Wrapped trees look like huge lollipops with **irregular** edges, rather than smooth, even ones.*

Look for context clues. What **Words That Mean the Opposite** can you find?

The words *rather than* are a clue. The words *smooth* and *even* are the opposite of *irregular*.

Think about the context clues and other information you may already know.

A lollipop has smooth, even, rounded edges. A tree wrapped in cloth would have uneven edges.

Predict a meaning for the word *irregular*.

The word *irregular* must mean "not smooth or even."

Check the dictionary to be sure of the meaning.

The word *irregular* means "not evenly shaped or arranged; uneven."

🔒 Unlock the Meanings

Practice the Strategy Here is one of the boldfaced words from the article on page 116. Use the context clues strategy on page 117 to figure out the meaning of the word.

luminous

📖 **Read** the sentence that uses the word *luminous* and some of the sentences around it.

🔍 **Look** for context clues. What **Words That Mean the Opposite** can you find?

_____

_____

_____

💡 **Think** about the context clues. What other helpful information do you know?

_____

_____

➡ **Predict** a meaning for the word *luminous*.

_____

_____

✔ **Check** the Word Wisdom Dictionary to be sure of the meaning. Write the meaning here.

_____

_____

_____

Use Context Clues The two words you have learned so far are checked off in the Word List. In the first column, write the other eight words from the Word List. Use context clues to predict a meaning for each word under "Your Prediction." Then look up the meaning in the Word Wisdom Dictionary. Write the dictionary meaning under "Dictionary Says."

WORD LIST

- permanent
- fabric
- formless
- dimension
- abstract
- synthetic
- ✔ irregular
- shimmer
- billow
- ✔ luminous

Vocabulary Word	Your Prediction	Dictionary Says
1		
2		
3		
4		
5		
6		
7		
8		

Process the Meanings

WORD LIST

permanent
fabric
formless
dimension
abstract
synthetic
irregular
shimmer
billow
luminous

Solve the Riddles   Write a word from the Word List to solve each riddle.

1 I am a measure of length, height, or width. What am I?

_____

2 I am a piece of art, but you can't tell exactly what I stand for. What am I?

_____

3 I am designed to last long into the future. What am I?

_____

4 I am used to make your clothing, and I start with the letter *f*. What am I?

_____

5 You won't find me in nature because I am made by human beings. I start with the letter *s*. What am I?

_____

Match the Descriptions   Write the word from the Word List that matches each description. Do not repeat any words that you used in the exercise above.

Two words that can describe shape are **6** _____

and **7** _____.

Two words that have something to do with the word *light* are

8 _____ and **9** _____.

A word that can describe how something moves is

10 _____.

Apply What You've Learned

Demonstrate Word Knowledge   Follow the directions or answer the questions.

1 List two things that could **shimmer**. _____

2 List two things that might **billow**. _____

3 List two kinds of cloth or material that are **synthetic**.

_____

4 List two things that have three **dimensions**.

_____

5 List two things that are **permanent**. _____

6 List two things that may be **abstract**. _____

_____

7 Name two things made of **fabric**. _____

_____

8 Name something that is **formless**. _____

9 Write two words that are the opposite of **luminous**.

_____

10 Name two things that can be **irregular**. _____

_____

Write It!   What is the most interesting or unusual piece of art you have ever seen? Describe it, using as many words from the Part 1 Word List as you can.

Latin Roots

for Word Wisdom

Keep Earth Beautiful:

Recycling Around the World

Young people throughout the United States are worried about the environment. They are not alone. School children around the world are doing their part to protect Earth. The whole world looks better without trash lying around.

Ghana is in Africa. Students there helped clean up their school grounds. They picked up trash and sorted it. They made sure the plastic, metal, and paper trash were placed in the **correct** bins so they could be recycled. The students placed trash cans around the school as a **direct** way to prevent littering. They also drew posters to **illustrate** the need to recycle.

Prince Edward Island is in Canada. Students there also collected and recycled trash. They **erected** a bulletin board for messages about caring for Earth. To spread this message, they chose the **format** of classroom visits. Pairs of students went to each class to explain how to recycle. The students also planted flower beds. The **formation** of the beds discourages students from walking across the lawns.

Nova Scotia is another area in Canada. One school there had a **rectangular** strip of unused land that was divided into **uniform** sections. Each section was given to a class. The classes grew plants native to the area and other plants that attract birds. Some gardens also included edible plants.

São Paulo is in Brazil. A river passes in front of a school there. Students studied an area of land along this river. They learned about its soil. Then they helped choose native trees that would grow there. The students wanted the trees to grow straight and healthy, not **deformed** or sick. They attended workshops to learn how to care for the trees. Then they helped plant 800 new trees.

Hungary is in Europe. Students there learned that lime trees once grew in their village, but they all died. The young people started a replanting project. In the end, they helped plant 419 trees and bushes. Lime trees now grow in their village again.

Young people around the world are working to protect Earth. When they talk about their projects, enthusiasm **illuminates** their faces. They want a cleaner and healthier world. They are willing to work to make it that way.

Practice the Context Clues Strategy Here is one of the boldfaced words from the essay on page 122. Use the context clues strategy you learned in Part 1 on page 117 to figure out the meaning of this word.

deformed

Read the sentence that uses the word *deformed* and some of the sentences around it.

Look for context clues to the word's meaning. What **Words That Mean the Opposite** can you find?

_____

_____

_____

Think about the context clues. What other helpful information do you know?

_____

_____

_____

Predict a meaning for the word *deformed*.

_____

_____

_____

Check your Word Wisdom Dictionary to be sure of the meaning of the word *deformed*. Write the definition here.

_____

_____

_____

Unlock the Meanings

Many words you use have Latin roots. Knowing the meanings of different roots can help you figure out the meaning of new words. Some words you learned in Part 1 have a Latin root. Each root relates to appearance.

Latin Root: **form**
meaning: a shape
English word: *formless*
meaning: without shape

Latin Root: **luc, lus, lum**
meaning: light, clear
English word: *luminous*
meaning: shining; full of light

Latin Root: **rect, reg**
meaning: to rule, straight
English word: *irregular*
meaning: without a regular shape

WORD LIST

correct
direct
illustrate
erect
format
formation
rectangular
uniform
deformed
illuminate

Sort by Roots Find these roots in the Word List. Write each word on a line under the correct root. Then think of other words you know that come from the same Latin roots. Write each word under the correct root.

Latin Root: form	Latin Root: luc, lus, lum	Latin Root: rect, reg

Appearance

Prefix	Meaning
ir-	not

Example

ir- (not) + **reg** (straight) + **-ular** (adj.) = **irregular**

Use Roots and Prefixes Circle the root and any prefix you find in the boldfaced words below. Use context clues, roots, and prefixes to write the meaning of the word. Check your definitions in the dictionary.

1 Please hold the flashlight to **illuminate** the dark closet.

_____

2 I want to **correct** some mistakes I made in this crossword puzzle.

_____

3 Who **illustrated** that book? The drawings are very beautiful.

_____

4 Most picture frames are **rectangular,** with the usual four right angles.

_____

5 What **format** will you use for the newsletter, two columns or three?

_____

6 All the tiles on the floor are **uniform**. None are different.

_____

7 The rock **formation** on that hillside looks like a person.

_____

8 Please tell me the most **direct** route to the museum.

_____

9 The town will **erect** a statue in front of the town hall.

_____

10 Jill's favorite doll has a **deformed** leg, but Jill doesn't mind.

_____

Process the Meanings

WORD LIST

- correct
- direct
- illustrate
- erect
- format
- formation
- rectangular
- uniform
- deformed
- illuminate

Match the Definitions Write the vocabulary word that matches each definition.

Definition	Vocabulary Word
1 to shine light on _____	format
2 to fix _____	correct
3 a pattern _____	illuminate
4 not winding around _____	erect
5 to draw _____	illustrate
6 to build _____	direct

Complete the Story Write the word from the Word List that best completes each sentence in the story. Do not repeat any of the words from the exercise above.

The artist scooped a handful of formless clay from a barrel. She had in mind the complete **7** _____ of the scene she would create. First, she rolled a few balls of clay that were all **8** _____ in size. Then she carefully shaped four-sided pieces, making **9** _____ bricks. After she finished her work, she joined the bricks to the other shapes.

After the artist left the room, her cat sat on the sculpture. The work was **10** _____! When she saw it, the artist sighed and tossed the clay back into the barrel. She would try again tomorrow.

Apply What You've Learned

Complete the Analogies Choose the word in parentheses that best completes each analogy. Write the word on the line.

1 Umbrella is to shade as candle is to _____
(illustrate, illuminate)

2 Destroy is to tear down as build is to _____
(erect, deformed)

3 Winding is to roundabout as straight is to _____
(correct, direct)

4 Town is to map as book is to _____
(format, illuminate)

5 Dirt is to wash as mistake is to _____
(correct, erect)

6 Writing is to print as drawing is to _____
(illustrate, format)

7 Hot is to cold as perfect is to _____
(direct, deformed)

Demonstrate Word Knowledge Follow the directions.

8 Give three examples of things that are **rectangular**.

_____

9 List three things that could be in **formation**.

_____

10 Give three examples of things that are **uniform**.

_____

Speak It! Tell a partner about an art project you once created or something you once built. Use as many words as you can from the Part 2 Word List.

PART 3

Reference Skills

for Word Wisdom

The Look of Fall:

Falling Colors

Do the trees change color every fall where you live? Have you admired the yellow, red, orange, and purple leaves that grace the trees when the weather turns cooler? Do you know why those leaves are no longer green?

The color change of fall leaves is triggered by shorter days and cooler temperatures. But the bright colors that appear in the leaves are not a **discoloration**. Those colors were there all along. They were covered up by a green pigment called chlorophyll. This pigment helps plants make their food. However, chlorophyll is **fragile**. It breaks down easily. The leaves must keep producing more of it. This process requires sunlight and warmth.

When autumn arrives, the leaves can no longer produce as much chlorophyll. However, the leaves still have other pigments. Xantho-phyll is a yellow pigment. It is more **sturdy** than chlorophyll. It does not break down as easily. Leaves with little chlorophyll and lots of xanthophyll are a **vivid** yellow.

Another pigment, called antho-cyanin, causes the red and purple in leaves. This pigment also makes apples red and grapes purple. Some kinds of trees, such as red oaks and red maples, produce a large amount of this pigment. They are very **decorative** in the fall, turning bright red and purple.

Some leaves have a pigment called carotene. In the fall, it makes the leaves turn orange. Carotene, along with xanthophyll, also makes carrots orange.

Leaf color is greatly affected by the weather. Low temperatures increase the anthocyanin in leaves, so maples turn bright red. Still, an early frost can cause a paler red. The best **clarity** of color results when dry, sunny days are followed by cool, dry nights. Too much rain or hot weather can cause the leaves to turn a **murky** color. Some leaves, such as those on oak trees, turn a **drab** brown every year. In fact, oak leaves do not drop in the fall. They can provide a **dense** cover for birds until new leaves start to grow in the spring.

As you travel through the coun-try, the bright colors of fall seem to be random, not **geometric**. However, each color change has a specific cause. The changing colors are one more amazing part of Mother Nature's plan.

Practice the Context Clues Strategy Here is one of the boldfaced words from the essay on page 128. Use the context clues strategy you learned in Part 1 on page 117 to figure out the meaning of this word.

geometric

Read the sentence that uses the word *geometric* and some of the sentences around it.

Look for context clues to the word's meaning. What **Words That Mean the Opposite** can you find?

_____

_____

_____

Think about the context clues. What other helpful information do you know?

_____

_____

_____

Predict a meaning for the word *geometric*.

_____

_____

_____

Check your Word Wisdom Dictionary to be sure of the meaning of the word *geometric*. Write the definition here.

_____

_____

_____

Pronunciation and Phonetic Respellings Every dictionary entry includes a phonetic respelling. The phonetic respelling tells you how to pronounce the word correctly.

The phonetic respelling also shows which syllable to stress (say with the most force). In words with several syllables, more than one syllable may be stressed.

Some dictionaries show the syllable with the primary stress (the most emphasis) in boldface with a boldfaced stress mark. The syllable with the next amount of stress is shown with a stress mark that is not boldfaced.

If a word has two correct pronunciations, both pronunciations will be shown. The first respelling shows the preferred way to pronounce the word.

Answer the Questions Use your Word Wisdom Dictionary to answer these questions.

1 Which two words in the Word List have more than one correct pronunciation?

_____

2 Does the preferred pronunciation of the word *fragile* have any stress on the second syllable?

_____

3 Which syllable has the most stress in the word *discoloration*?

_____

4 Which syllable has secondary stress (some stress) in the word *discoloration*?

_____

5 Which letter is silent in *decorative*?

_____

Find the Meaning
1. Use context clues.
2. Look for a familiar root, prefix, or suffix.
3. If the context or a word part doesn't help, check the dictionary.

Define the Words Follow the steps above to write the meaning of each boldfaced word. Write 1, 2, or 3 to show which steps you used.

WORD LIST

discoloration
fragile
sturdy
vivid
decorative
clarity
murky
drab
dense
geometric

1 Army uniforms are made in **drab** colors so they aren't easily seen.

_____

2 The ancient Incas drew huge **geometric** designs on the earth.

_____

3 Be sure to wear **sturdy** shoes when you go hiking in the desert.

_____

4 Mr. George explains his ideas with **clarity**, so we understand.

_____

5 The pond was **murky**, making it hard to see the bottom.

_____

6 I have a **vivid** memory of my first time in an airplane.

_____

7 The **discoloration** on my jeans is from bleach.

_____

8 The pictures of fish made the shower curtain **decorative**.

_____

9 The fog was so **dense** that we did not see the bus arrive.

_____

10 Butterflies seem so **fragile**, but they fly hundreds of miles.

_____

Process the Meanings

WORD LIST

discoloration

fragile

sturdy

vivid

decorative

clarity

murky

drab

dense

geometric

Choose the Antonyms Write the word from the Word List that means the opposite of the underlined word or words and fits the context of the sentence.

1 That glass vase is very <u>strong</u>. _____

2 Aren't the colors in that painting <u>dull</u>? _____

3 This city is <u>not crowded</u> with people. _____

4 The river was <u>clear</u> after the storm. _____

5 I dress in <u>bright</u> colors when I feel sad. _____

Rewrite the Sentences Rewrite each sentence, using the word in parentheses.

6 We put up wallpaper that was very colorful. (decorative)

_____

7 I stood on a strong ladder to reach the ceiling. (sturdy)

_____

8 The paper had a pattern of lines and shapes. (geometric)

_____

9 One roll of wallpaper had some places where the color did not match the rest. (discoloration)

_____

_____

10 The design on that roll did not have the same clear lines and colors as on the other rolls. (clarity)

_____

_____

Apply What You've Learned

Relate the Meanings Answer the questions or follow the directions.

1 Would a house with glass walls be **sturdy**? Explain.

_____

2 Describe a time that you were out in **murky** weather.

_____

3 Do you like to wear **drab** clothing?

_____

4 What could cause **discoloration** of your clothing?

_____

5 What could you do to make your classroom more **decorative**?

_____

6 Describe something that has a **geometric** design.

_____

7 Describe something in your classroom that is **fragile**.

_____

8 Describe a **vivid** dream you once had.

_____

9 How could you explain something with great **clarity**?

_____

10 Describe a setting or a location that you know is **dense**.

_____

Write It! If you could decorate a room, how would you do it? Use several Part 3 vocabulary words.

Review

for Word Wisdom

WORD LIST

permanent
fabric
formless
dimension
abstract
synthetic
irregular
shimmer
billow
luminous
correct
direct
illustrate
erect
format
formation
rectangular
uniform
deformed
illuminate
discoloration
fragile
sturdy
vivid
decorative
clarity
murky
drab
dense
geometric

Sort by Parts of Speech Sort the words in the Word List by part of speech. Write each word in the correct column of the chart. If a word can be used as more than one part of speech, write the word under more than one column. Then, circle the words that have the roots *form, luc, lus, lum, rect,* or *reg.*

Nouns	Verbs	Adjectives

Identify the Synonyms and Antonyms Read each pair of words. Write **S** if the words are synonyms. Write **A** if the words are antonyms.

_____ **1** dense   murky

_____ **2** rectangular   geometric

_____ **3** sturdy   fragile

_____ **4** vivid   drab

_____ **5** formless   irregular

Demonstrate Word Knowledge Answer the questions or follow the directions.

6 Give the **dimensions** of something on your desk or in the room.

_____

7 Describe what might cause **discoloration** of **fabric**.

_____

_____

8 How could you **illuminate** a place that is **dense** with fog so that you could see with more **clarity**?

_____

_____

9 Describe the **format** of this page in your book.

_____

_____

10 Look around you. Describe something **decorative**.

_____

Taking Vocabulary Tests

TEST-TAKING STRATEGY

Some tests are scored by a machine. Be sure to fill in your answers in the correct way. You don't want to lose points because you didn't fill in an answer bubble completely or because you filled in two bubbles by mistake. If you fill in two answers—even if one is right—the machine will score it as incorrect. If you erase, be sure to erase completely.

Sample:

It is dark outside this afternoon. The clouds are **murky**. It will probably rain soon.

The word **murky** means

_____.

- ◉ gloomy
- ○ sunny
- ○ bright
- ○ blue

Practice Test   Read the paragraph. Then fill in the answer bubble for each statement.

1 Gail measured the **fabric** for her costume carefully before cutting it. **2** She didn't want to have to **correct** any mistakes. **3** The light cloth would **billow** around her when she moved. **4** She would add sparkling beads for a **decorative** touch. **5** With clouds, twinkling stars, and a silvery moon, her costume would certainly not look **drab**.

1 The word **fabric** means _____.
- ○ fashion
- ○ color
- ○ cloth
- ○ design

2 The word **correct** means _____.
- ○ fill
- ○ fix
- ○ save
- ○ add

3 The word **billow** means _____.
- ○ sit
- ○ dream
- ○ sleep
- ○ flutter

4 The word **decorative** means _____.
- ○ funny
- ○ sticky
- ○ unusual
- ○ fancy

5 The word **drab** means _____.
- ○ dull
- ○ bright
- ○ green
- ○ simple

Do a Multiple-Meaning Crossword Puzzle Each clue below gives two meanings for a vocabulary word. Read the clues. Then write the vocabulary word in the correct space.

DOWN

1 to fix; right

3 to light up; to make clear

5 a design or plan; to make a plan

ACROSS

2 to lead; straight

4 uneven; not usual

6 standing straight; to put up

7 work clothing; all alike

8 arrangement; act of making something

Speak It! Choose four or five vocabulary words from this unit to describe something that you can see right now.

PART 1

Context Clues

for Word Wisdom

Good Advice:

Ask Ms. Know It

Do you know how to act properly in social settings? Not everyone does, but anyone can learn. Read these letters to see what the "expert" has to say.

Relationships

UNIT 7

1

Dear Ms. Know It,

I never know what to do in polite **society**. I'm **familiar** with some basic rules of good behavior, like saying "please" and "thank you." However, I have many other questions. For example, which fork is **appropriate** to use with my salad? Is it **considerate** to hold a door open for other people?

I would feel more **confident** if I knew how to act. My **maternal** grandmother says I should do what my mother did and read a good book about manners. Please help.

Sincerely,
Confused

2

Dear Confused,

A dose of good manners never hurts. Don't **isolate** yourself from others just because you don't know a few simple rules for good behavior. It is really **admirable** that you want to improve yourself. Knowing how to act can make you feel very confident, and you may even find new friends and become more **popular**.

Just read my book, *Thirty Days to Magnificent Manners*. It will teach you everything you need to know.

Sincerely,
Ms. Know It

3

Dear Ms. Know It,

I read your book from cover to cover. I now know how to act in any social situation. I'm writing to tell you that I have more confidence, and I have started to **involve** myself in many new activities. I have even been elected president of our Student Council. I owe it all to you.

Sincerely,
Formerly Confused

Context Clues Strategy

Look for Words Related to the Word

EXAMPLE: When you hurt someone's feelings, offer an *apology* and a handshake.

CLUE: The word *When* is a clue. *Hurt someone's feelings* and *a handshake* are related to the word *apology*. They tell why you might feel sorry about something and what you might do about it. These words help you to understand what *apology* means.

Here are steps for using this context clues strategy to figure out the meaning of the word *involve*, which appeared in one of the letters you just read.

Read the sentence with the unknown word and some of the sentences around it.

*I'm writing to tell you that I have more confidence, and I have started to **involve** myself in many new activities. I have even been elected president of our Student Council.*

Look for context clues. What **Words Related to the Word** can you find?

The new activities and club presidency show that this person is participating in many things.

Think about the context clues and other helpful information you know.

My mother always says that my sister is involved in too many sports activities.

Predict a meaning for the word.

Involve must mean "to participate in something."

Check your dictionary to be sure of the meaning.

Involve means "to include or draw in."

Unlock the Meanings

Practice the Strategy Here is one of the boldfaced words from the letters on page 138. Use the context clues strategy on page 139 to figure out the meaning of the word.

maternal

Read the sentence that uses the word *maternal* and some of the sentences around it.

Look for context clues. What **Words Related to the Word** can you find?

_____

_____

_____

Think about the context clues. What other helpful information do you know?

_____

_____

_____

Predict a meaning for the word *maternal*.

_____

_____

_____

Check a dictionary to be sure of the meaning of the word *maternal*. Which of the meanings for the word *maternal* fits the context?

_____

_____

society		
familiar		
appropriate		
considerate		
confident		
✔ maternal		
isolate		
admirable		
popular		
✔ involve		

Use Context Clues   The two words you have already been introduced to are checked off in the Word List. In the first column, write the other eight boldfaced words from the Word List. In the second column, predict the meaning for each word. Then look up the meaning in a dictionary. In the third column, write the dictionary meaning that fits the context.

	Vocabulary Word	Your Prediction	Dictionary Says
1			
2			
3			
4			
5			
6			
7			
8			

Process the Meanings

WORD LIST

society

familiar

appropriate

considerate

confident

maternal

isolate

admirable

popular

involve

Match the Descriptions Write the word from the Word List that best matches each description.

1 people who act in a motherly way:_____

2 people who are sure of themselves:_____

3 people who have many friends:_____

4 people who deserve approval and respect:

_____

5 people who care about the feelings of others:

_____

6 people whom you know well: _____

Complete the Sentences Choose the word from the Word List that best completes each sentence. Do not repeat any of the answers you used above.

7 When you take part in an event, you _____ yourself in it.

8 All people are a part of the _____ in which they live.

9 If you choose not to spend any time with others, you

_____ yourself.

10 If you know how to act in all kinds of situations, your

behavior is always_____

Apply What You've Learned

Demonstrate Word Knowledge Use what you know about the boldfaced words to answer the questions. Use complete sentences.

1 Does being **confident** help make people more **popular**? Why or why not?

_____

_____

2 How could people who are **isolated** get more **involved** in their community?

_____

_____

3 Why would someone need to be **familiar** with you to act in a **maternal** way toward you?

_____

_____

4 Do you think **considerate** people are **admirable**? Why or why not?

_____

_____

5 What is one public behavior that **society** considers **appropriate**?

_____

_____

Write It! Think about your own community and about our country. Write about something you would like to change about our society. Use as many vocabulary words from Part 1 as you can.

PART 2 Latin Roots

for Word Wisdom

Elephant Grandmothers:
They Know Best

Many animals live in groups. They form families, much like humans. However, not all animal families are the same.

Lions form **social** groups called prides. A pride is led by the strongest male, who is the **patriarch**. In elephant families, however, the oldest female is in charge. She is the **matriarch**. Elephant families are based on maternal links, not **paternal** links. An elephant family consists of a matriarch, about six other females, and their babies. When the males become adults, they live away from the female groups. Males have contact with females only at mating time.

Elephant family groups often feed near each other. Some groups feel safe together. Still, families avoid groups they do not know. An older matriarch—like a grandmother elephant—can tell when a strange group is approaching. She draws her family close together. A younger matriarch cannot easily tell a friend from a foe. She groups her family together too often and doesn't feel safe. As a result, she will have fewer babies. She has a lower **maternity** rate than females led by older matriarchs.

Killing elephants is against the law. Yet poachers still hunt them. Few large males are left. Some poachers now kill the females. Yet killing an old female can mean more than the death of one animal. The loss of a matriarch can weaken the entire elephant **population**.

Hunting is not the only danger that elephants face. Conflicts also arise when they roam onto **public** land. Some invade small farms. They destroy crops as they search for food. A number of **associations** work to protect elephants. One is the Born Free Foundation in Kenya. This group helped move about fifty elephants to Meru National Park. There, they could be protected. The elephants were moved by truck, one by one. Once released, they soon found their family members. At the park, the families have a better life. They roam over thousands of acres of protected land.

Publicity about the move has helped. Now more people want to help the elephants. Park **patrons** can watch the elephant families. Yet elephants are still at risk. The matriarchs can only do so much to keep their families safe.

Practice the Context Clues Strategy Here is one
of the boldfaced words from the essay on page 144. Use
the context clues strategy you learned in Part 1 on page
139 to figure out the meaning of this word.

associations

Read the sentence that uses the word *associations* and
some of the sentences around it.

Look for context clues to the word's meaning. What
Words Related to the Word can you find?

_____

_____

_____

Think about the context clues and other information you
may already know.

_____

_____

_____

Predict a meaning for the word *associations*.

_____

_____

_____

Check your Word Wisdom Dictionary to be sure of the
meaning of the word *association*. Write the definition here.

_____

_____

Unlock the Meanings

Knowing the meanings of different roots will help you figure out the meaning of many new words. Several words you learned in Part 1 have Latin roots. These roots are related to relationships.

Latin Root: **pop, pub**
meaning: people
English word: *popular*
meaning: having many friends

Latin Root: **soci**
meaning: companion
English word: *society*
meaning: people living together

Latin Root: **mat, matr**
meaning: mother
English word: *maternal*
meaning: related to motherhood

Latin Root: **pat, patr**
meaning: father
English word: *patriot*
meaning: loyal citizen

Sort by Roots Find the Latin roots you just learned in the Word List. Write each word in the correct column. Think of other words you know that have these roots. Write them in the correct column.

WORD LIST

- social
- patriarch
- matriarch
- paternal
- maternity
- population
- public
- association
- publicity
- patron

Latin Root: pop, pub	Latin Root: soci	Latin Root: mat, matr	Latin Root: pat, patr

Relationships

Prefix	Meaning
as-	to, toward

Example

as- (toward) + soci (companion) + -ation (noun)
= **association**

Use Roots and Prefixes Circle any root and prefix you find in the boldfaced words. Then write the meaning of each word.

1 Everyone in that **association** is a cat lover.

_____

2 The **matriarch** sat at the head of the table surrounded by her family.

_____

3 Many people in entertainment like a lot of **publicity**.

_____

4 Dad and I are both named after my **paternal** grandfather.

_____

5 The town's **population** has grown in the past ten years.

_____

6 Mom and the new baby are on the **maternity** floor of the hospital.

_____

7 We enjoy **social** events, because we like being with people.

_____

8 My great-grandfather is the **patriarch** of our family.

_____

9 Where is the nearest **public** library?

_____

10 Are you a **patron** of the new store on Elm Street?

_____

WORD LIST

- social
- patriarch
- matriarch
- paternal
- maternity
- population
- public
- association
- publicity
- patron

Complete the Ads Write the word from the Word List that is missing from each help-wanted ad.

1 Nurses are needed in the _____

department of the hospital. Must be good with babies.

2 A creative writer is needed to write ads and get good

_____ for a new company.

3 A male actor at least 65 years old is needed to play the

part of a _____ of a large family.

4 A _____ director is needed to plan

children's fun after-school activities.

5 An experienced coach is needed right away to lead

a(n) _____ of sports fans.

Use the Clues Use the clues to write a word from the Word List.

6 A school that is open to everyone is called this.

_____

7 Stores need this, which is another word for *shopper*.

_____

8 If someone is like this, he acts in a fatherly way.

_____

9 She is the head of her family. _____

10 It is larger in big cities than it is in small towns.

_____

Apply What You've Learned

Demonstrate Word Knowledge Answer the questions.

1 What could a restaurant do to get more **patrons**?

_____

2 What might you hear on the **maternity** floor of a hospital?

_____

3 Name an **association** or one you would like to start.

_____

4 What must one be to become a **matriarch**?

_____

5 What could you do to get **publicity** for a book fair?

_____

6 Whom do you consider a **patriarch** of the United States?

_____

7 How could you figure out the student **population** of your school?

_____

8 Name a favorite **social** event.

_____

9 Who is the son of your **paternal** grandfather?

_____

10 Which **public** building is closest to your home?

_____

 **Speak It!** Prepare a two-minute speech to convince the class to join a club. Use words from the Part 2 Word List.

Reference Skills

for Word Wisdom

Fun for All Ages:

A Letter for the Community Center

Dear Editor of the *Glenville Gazette*:

I am responding to Pat White's letter of June 20. White wrote that our town should not build a community center. He thought it was just too expensive. White was wrong, and I'll explain why.

This community has no good places for young people to **congregate**. Too many of them end up at the mall. The City Center Mall now has a **reputation** for being a hangout for troublemakers. Just last week, **rival** groups got into a scuffle there. I know a lot of my neighbors used to make it a **custom** to shop at the mall. Now they go to stores in the suburbs.

The kids at the mall just don't have anyplace else to go and be together. If we had a community center, they could play basketball, swim, or play video games in a safer setting. A community center could offer group and **individual** activities for all ages.

The last town my family lived in had a community center. I can tell you from **personal** experience that it was a fun place to go. The center offered all kinds of classes. For example, my little brother took a class in caring for pets and other **domestic** animals. My dad took a class in working with stained glass. My mom loved her aerobics class. If you wanted **privacy,** the center had quiet places to sit and read. If you wanted action, there were all kinds of games and teams. **Participation** was so popular that many classes and teams had a long waiting list.

It's true that twenty million dollars is a huge amount to spend on a community center. Our town does have other needs. Perhaps the people who want the center and those who don't want it could **compromise**. Maybe the center could be built in stages, or we could do without some parts, like a climbing wall.

I strongly urge the town to find a way to fund a community center. We all need it, especially our young people.

Sincerely,

Joyce Wilkins

Practice the Context Clues Strategy Here is one of the boldfaced words from the letter to the editor on page 150. Use the context clues strategy you learned in Part 1 on page 139 to figure out the meaning of this word.

privacy

📖 **Read** the sentence that uses the word *privacy* and some of the sentences around it.

🔍 **Look** for context clues to the word's meaning. What **Words Related to the Word** can you find?

_____

_____

_____

💡 **Think** about the context clues and other information you may already know.

_____

_____

_____

➡️ **Predict** a meaning for the word *privacy*.

_____

_____

_____

✔️ **Check** your Word Wisdom Dictionary to be sure of the meaning of the word *privacy*. Write the meaning here.

_____

_____

_____

🔑 Unlock the Meanings

The Internet   The Internet is a useful tool for finding information. You can quickly find information you need by carefully choosing key words for your search. If your key words are too general, you will get links that you don't need. If your key words are too narrow, you may not find the most helpful articles.

Here are tips for finding information on the Internet:

1. Always let an adult know when you are using the Internet. Never give out any information about yourself, such as your phone number, address, or school.

2. Type in only the most important words in your search topic. Leave out words like *the, and,* and *of.*

3. When writing a report, print the Internet page with the useful information. The Web site address will appear on the bottom of the page. Use this address to go back to the site or to list the article in your bibliography.

4. Be sure the source is trustworthy. Just because the information is given on the Internet doesn't make it true.

Practice Using Key Words   Write at least two key words that you could use to search the Internet for information on these topics.

1 domestic birds

_____

2 college football rivals

_____

3 individual rights

_____

4 the World Series

_____

5 wedding customs

_____

Find the Meaning
1. Use context clues.
2. Look for a familiar root, prefix, or suffix.
3. If the context or a word part doesn't help, check the dictionary.

Define the Words Follow the steps above to write the meaning for each boldfaced word. Write 1, 2, or 3 to show which steps you used.

WORD LIST

congregate
reputation
rival
custom
individual
personal
domestic
privacy
participation
compromise

1 During recess, the students **congregate** around the swings.

_____

2 The two sides each gave up something in the **compromise**.

_____

3 Our class had the highest **participation** in the bake sale.

_____

4 What subject in school is your **personal** favorite?

_____

5 Cats and dogs are **domestic** animals.

_____

6 I know Shay will be my biggest **rival** for class president.

_____

7 If you want **privacy**, keep your door closed.

_____

8 Do you prefer **individual** or group activities?

_____

9 I have a **reputation** as a great speller.

_____

10 My family has the **custom** of painting eggs each spring.

_____

WORD LIST

- congregate
- reputation
- rival
- custom
- individual
- personal
- domestic
- privacy
- participation
- compromise

Complete the Analogies Write the vocabulary word that best completes each analogy.

1 Group is to crowd as _____ is to person.

2 Law is to government as _____ is to culture.

3 Wolf is to wild as dog is to _____.

4 Day is to night as friend is to _____.

Rewrite the Sentences Rewrite each sentence. Use the word in parentheses in your sentence.

5 After a long talk, we reached an agreement. (compromise)

_____

6 I like to keep my thoughts and feelings to myself. (privacy)

_____

7 Could you do this favor just for me? (personal)

_____

8 Every Fourth of July we get together in the park for a picnic. (congregate)

_____

9 People think of me as a loyal friend. (reputation)

_____

10 The hospital hopes that many people will take part in the blood drive. (participation)

_____

Apply What You've Learned

Link to Your Life Follow the directions or answer the questions.

1 How could you turn a **rival** into a friend? _____

_____

2 Tell of a time when you want **privacy**. _____

_____

3 Name an animal that can't be a **domestic** pet. Explain why.

_____

4 How could someone strengthen his **reputation**?

_____

5 Describe a time you reached a **compromise** with someone.

_____

6 Describe a **custom** that you enjoy. _____

_____

7 Describe your favorite place to **congregate** with friends.

_____

8 How could you encourage **participation** in a recycling program?

_____

9 What sport requires **individual** effort? _____

_____

10 What **personal** objects would you take on a trip? _____

_____

Write It! Do you think it is important to join after-school clubs or play sports? Write two paragraphs telling why or why not. Use as many vocabulary words from Part 3 as you can.

Review

for Word Wisdom

WORD LIST

- society
- familiar
- appropriate
- considerate
- confident
- maternal
- isolate
- admirable
- popular
- involve
- social
- patriarch
- matriarch
- paternal
- maternity
- population
- public
- association
- publicity
- patron
- congregate
- reputation
- rival
- custom
- individual
- personal
- domestic
- privacy
- participation
- compromise

Sort by Syllables Say each word in the Word List. Sort the words by the number of syllables in the word. Write each word in the correct column. Then circle the words that have these roots: *pop, pub, soci, mat, matr, pat, patr*.

②Syllables	③Syllables	④Syllables	⑤Syllables

Match the Words and Meanings Write the letter of the correct meaning in column B next to each word in column A.

Column A	Column B
1 reputation _____	a. taking part in
2 congregate _____	b. thoughtful
3 considerate _____	c. habit
4 involve _____	d. how people think of you
5 association _____	e. to include
6 admirable _____	f. time alone
7 participation _____	g. tame
8 domestic _____	h. deserving praise
9 custom _____	i. to gather
10 privacy _____	j. organization
11 appropriate _____	k. news given out to get attention
12 personal _____	l. including people
13 publicity _____	m. proper
14 social _____	n. female head of a family
15 matriarch _____	o. relating to one person
16 familiar _____	p. a regular customer
17 individual _____	q. male head of a family
18 patriarch _____	r. single
19 isolate _____	s. having knowledge of
20 patron _____	t. to separate

Review

TEST-TAKING STRATEGY

If you have trouble answering a test question, go on to the next one. That way you won't waste too much time. Put a light pencil mark next to the one you skip over. If you use a separate answer sheet, make sure to skip the matching answer space as well. After you finish the rest of the test, come back to the question you skipped and try it again. Be sure to erase any extra pencil marks you made.

Sample:

good publicity
O standing
O friend
⊙ news
O meal

Practice Test Fill in the circle of the answer choice that shows the correct meaning for the underlined word.

1 maternal feelings
O childish
O fatherly
O warm
O motherly

2 individual serving
O small
O large
O extra
O single

3 isolate a patient
O separate from others
O operate on
O take care of
O give medicine to

4 reach a compromise
O decision
O agreement
O conclusion
O obstacle

5 feel confident
O smart
O angry
O sure
O silly

6 parent association
O dinner
O meeting
O letter
O group

7 business patron
O office
O worker
O customer
O owner

8 familiar place
O friendly
O well-known
O unknown
O lonely

9 considerate act
O thoughtful
O selfish
O thoughtless
O original

10 popular restaurant
O expensive
O well-liked
O foreign
O family

Build New Words

Write the Parts of Speech Some words can be more than one part of speech. Read these examples:

That doctor offers excellent <u>maternity</u> care to his patients. **(adjective)**

Her <u>maternity</u> began with the birth of her first child. **(noun)**

Read each sentence below. Then write **noun, verb,** or **adjective** on the line to show what part of speech the boldfaced word is. If necessary, use your Word Wisdom Dictionary.

1 We enjoyed walking in the **public** garden. _____

This museum is open to the **public** every day. _____

2 After a long discussion the two groups reached a **compromise**.

_____

Are you usually willing to **compromise** when you and a friend

disagree? _____

3 The snacks are packaged in **individual** servings. _____

My cousin is a very happy **individual**. _____

4 Bill is Harry's biggest **rival**. _____

Those teams **rival** each other in scoring ability. _____

5 Lynn gave an **appropriate** response. _____

They will **appropriate** money for the project. _____

Speak It! Choose a partner and role-play a telephone conversation about your day at school. Discuss who you saw, what you discussed in class, and any activities you took part in. The events can be real or imaginary. Use as many words from this unit as you can.

Good and Bad

PART 1

Context Clues

for Word Wisdom

How Wisdom Defeated an Army:

Carcassonne

In the south of France there is an ancient city that is now a major tourist attraction. The following legend tells about the early days of Carcassonne (pronounced /kär•kä•sôn′/) and how it got its name.

More than 1,000 years ago, the land that is now France was a wild, untamed place. Charlemagne, a fierce leader, tried to **conquer** many people. His armies roamed the country **invading** villages, entering, and fighting for control.

It is said that Charlemagne's soldiers arrived at a walled castle. The people within the walls had drawn up the gate. Charlemagne's soldiers laid **siege** to the castle, but its walls were well defended. The soldiers decided that if they waited long enough, the people in the castle would starve or surrender.

The people in the castle knew they would need to **conserve** their supplies of food and grain to make them last until the siege was over. They were **determined** not to give up their castle.

Weeks passed and then months and then years. Within the castle walls, the people were growing hungry. They knew they would be **desperate** for food soon.

A woman named Madame Carcas tried to **reassure** the people. "I have a plan," she calmly announced. "We need not give in to our **misfortune.**" She asked the people to bring her their last bits of grain. The people were **astonished** when Madame Carcas ordered that the grain be fed to a pig!

Then she ordered that the pig be thrown over the castle wall. It landed near the soldiers, who saw that it was fat with grain. The soldiers **assumed** that if the people of the castle had enough food to be able to feed their animals, the people must be well supplied indeed! It could be many more years before the people would have to surrender.

The soldiers finally gave up and left. To celebrate, Madame Carcas ordered that the bells of the castle tower be rung. In French, the word *sonne* means "ring" as in "ring the bells." That is how the city of Carcassonne got its name. *Carcas sonne* means "(Madame) Carcas rings (the bells)."

Context Clues Strategy

Look for How Something Is Done

EXAMPLE: The people clapped and cheered loudly as they *rejoiced*.

CLUE: The words *clapped and cheered loudly* tell how the people *rejoiced*.

Here is another strategy for using context clues to understand new words. We use it here to understand *reassure* from the essay.

Read the sentence with the unknown word and some of the sentences around it.

*A woman named Madame Carcas tried to **reassure** the people. "I have a plan," she announced calmly.*

Look for context clues. What clues showing **How Something Is Done** can you find?

The words *calmly announced* tell how Madame Carcas *reassured* the people.

Think about the context clues and other helpful information you know.

When I feel scared and someone talks to me in a calm voice, I feel less nervous.

Predict a meaning for the word.

The word *reassure* probably means "to make others feel better about something."

Check a dictionary to be sure of the meaning.

The word *reassure* means "to restore confidence."

🔑 Unlock the Meanings

Practice the Strategy Here is one of the boldfaced words from the essay on page 160. Use the context clues strategy on page 161 to figure out the meaning of the word.

invading

📖 **Read** the sentence that uses the word *invading* and some of the sentences around it.

🔍 **Look** for context clues. What clues showing **How Something Is Done** can you find?

_____

_____

💡 **Think** about the context clues. What other helpful information do you know?

_____

_____

➤ **Predict** a meaning for the word *invading*.

_____

_____

✔ **Check** a dictionary to be sure of the meaning of the word *invade*. Which of the meanings for the word *invade* fits the context?

_____

_____

WORD LIST
conquer
✔ invade
siege
conserve
determined
desperate
✔ reassure
misfortune
astonish
assume

Use Context Clues You have been introduced to two vocabulary words from the essay on page 160. Those words are checked off in the Word List. Under "Vocabulary Word" write the other eight words from the Word List. Predict a meaning for each word under "Your Prediction." Then look up the meanings in the Word Wisdom Dictionary and write the definition under "Dictionary Says."

	Vocabulary Word	Your Prediction	Dictionary Says
1			
2			
3			
4			
5			
6			
7			
8			

Process the Meanings

WORD LIST

- conquer
- invade
- siege
- conserve
- determined
- desperate
- reassure
- misfortune
- astonish
- assume

Complete the Story Write the best word from the Word List to go in each blank. You will have to add an ending to one word.

The racer was **1** _____ to ski down the steep slope without falling. She had promised herself that she would **2** _____ her fear of hurting herself. Last season, she had the **3** _____ of breaking her leg. Now she tried to **4** _____ herself that she would not be hurt again.

At the bottom of the slope, she was **5** _____ when she saw her time on the race clock. She had skied without falling, and she had won!

Use the Clues Choose the word from the Word List that matches each clue. Write the word on the line.

6 This is how you may feel when you are very anxious about something. _____

7 This is what you do so that you won't run out of something. _____

8 This is what you do when you believe something without making sure that it is true. _____

9 This is what armies at war do to countries they want to defeat. _____

10 This is another name for an attack. _____

Apply What You've Learned

Answer the questions.

1 What kind of **misfortune** has a friend experienced?

_____

2 Has your bedroom ever looked as if a **siege** had taken place?

_____

3 When was a time when you were very **determined**?

_____

4 When have you ever been **desperate** for some water?

_____

5 Would you be **astonished** if a clown jumped out of a big cake?

_____

6 How could you **conserve** your energy if you got lost outdoors?

_____

7 What would you do if an army of ants **invaded** your picnic?

_____

8 If you were afraid of snakes, how could you **conquer** that fear?

_____

9 How would you **reassure** a young child who had a scary dream?

_____

10 When have you **assumed** something but were wrong?

_____

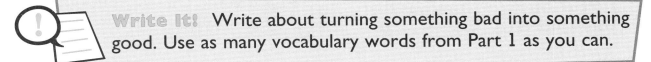

Write It! Write about turning something bad into something good. Use as many vocabulary words from Part 1 as you can.

PART

2

Latin Roots

for Word Wisdom

Do You Feel Lucky?

Good Luck Charms

Do you have any lucky charms? Do they improve your luck? Have you wondered why people find certain things lucky?

You might have heard that four-leaf clovers and horse-shoes are symbols of good luck. Here are some symbols that you might not know.

Pigs are thought to be symbols of good **fortune** in many cultures. In Germany, people often compliment others on their good luck with an expression that means "You have pig." Some Native American groups consider the pig to be a symbol of abundance. The pig reminds them to celebrate life and share what they have.

According to an Irish myth, the Celtic god of the sea kept a special herd of pigs. When these pigs were eaten, they appeared again. The gods ate the pigs as a way to **preserve** themselves. By eating the pigs, the gods would never grow old.

Rabbits are also a symbol of good luck. They are linked with spring and the growth of flowers. Seeing a rabbit run through your fields is a **fortuitous** sign. It means that your garden will grow well. (Of course, then the rabbit will have many **pleasant** meals!)

According to a German myth, the rabbit was once a bird. This **unfortunate** bird nearly died from the winter cold. The goddess of spring changed the bird into a rabbit. The rabbit brought rainbow eggs, a sign of spring.

Frogs are a symbol of abundance because they lay so many eggs. The Romans thought that frogs could bring good luck and **security** to their homes. The Irish people believed that frogs were related to leprechauns. If frogs were ever **displeased,** they would play tricks on you. In China, the three-legged toad was a pet of the god of wealth. This toad was often shown with a coin in its mouth.

Elephants are said to keep bad luck away. Some people place an elephant statue at every door of their homes. They believe that this animal brings **pleasure** and happiness into their lives. Elephants are also symbols of wisdom and strength. In ancient Asia and India, only kings **deserved** to ride them.

Are you feeling a little **insecure**? Perhaps a pig, rabbit, frog, or elephant could change your outlook and your luck!

Practice the Context Clues Strategy   Here is one of the boldfaced words from the essay on page 166. Use the context clues strategy you learned in Part 1 on page 161 to figure out the meaning of this word.

preserve

Read the sentence that uses the word *preserve* and some of the sentences around it.

Look for context clues to the word's meaning. What clues showing **How Something Is Done** can you find?

_____

_____

_____

Think about the context clues. What other helpful information do you know?

_____

_____

Predict a meaning for the word *preserve*.

_____

_____

_____

Check your Word Wisdom Dictionary to be sure of the meaning of the word *preserve*. Which of the meanings for the word fits the context?

_____

_____

_____

🔑 Unlock the Meanings

Knowing the meanings of different roots can help you figure out the meaning of new words. Several words you learned in Part 1 have a Latin root. Each root below is related to something good or bad.

> Latin Root: **cur, sur**
> meaning: to care
> English word: *reassure*
> meaning: to restore confidence

> Latin Root: **fortu**
> meaning: chance
> English word: *misfortune*
> meaning: bad luck

> Latin Root: **plea**
> meaning: to please
> English word: *pleasing*
> meaning: giving enjoyment

> Latin Root: **serv**
> meaning: to save, to serve
> English word: *conserve*
> meaning: to use carefully and without wasting

WORD LIST

- fortune
- preserve
- fortuitous
- pleasant
- unfortunate
- security
- displease
- pleasure
- deserve
- insecure

Sort by Roots Find these roots in the Word List. Write each word under the correct root. Circle the roots *cur*, *sur*, *fortu*, *plea*, and *serv*.

Good and Bad

Latin Root: **cur, sur**

_____

_____

Latin Root: **plea**

_____

_____

_____

Latin Root: **fortu**

_____

_____

_____

Latin Root: **serv**

_____

_____

Prefix	Meaning
un-	not
pre-	before

Example

un- (not) + **fortu** (chance) + **-nate** (adj.)
= **unfortunate**

Use Roots and Prefixes Circle the root and any prefix you find in the boldfaced words below. Use context clues, roots, and prefixes to write the meaning of each word.

1 Some people in the 1800s earned a **fortune** during the gold rush.

_____

2 It's always a **pleasure** to see you.

_____

3 It's **unfortunate** that Mandy had the flu on her birthday.

_____

4 Ty sounded **insecure** when he asked if there was a math test today.

_____

5 My mother pressed some roses in a heavy book to **preserve** them.

_____

6 The weather is usually **pleasant** here in September.

_____

7 Do you get a feeling of **security** by sleeping with a favorite blanket?

_____

8 Your driving by when we got a flat tire was **fortuitous**.

_____

9 You **deserve** a vacation since you have been working so hard.

_____

10 People who litter **displease** me more than almost anything.

_____

Process the Meanings

WORD LIST

fortune
preserve
fortuitous
pleasant
unfortunate
security
displease
pleasure
deserve
insecure

Complete the Analogies Read each analogy and the two vocabulary words in parentheses. Write the word that completes the analogy.

1 Trash is to discard as memories are to (deserve, preserve).

_____

2 Friend is to please as enemy is to (displease, pleasant).

_____

3 Frown is to unhappiness as smile is to (pleasant, pleasure). _____

4 Joke is to laughter as seatbelt is to (security, insecure).

_____

5 Debt is to poverty as money is to (fortune, unfortunate).

_____

Connect the Words Write the best word from the Word List to complete each sentence.

6 Breaking your leg would be very _____.

7 If you earn something, you _____ it.

8 Climbing stairs with no handrail could make someone feel

_____.

9 Most people enjoy being around those who are

_____.

10 A lucky break is _____.

Apply What You've Learned

Link to Your Life Use what you've learned to follow the directions.

1 Describe something that gives you great **pleasure.** _____

_____

2 Describe a time when you felt **insecure.** _____

_____

3 Describe a **pleasant** memory. _____

_____

4 Describe something that gives you a sense of **security.** _____

_____

5 Describe something you feel you **deserve.** _____

_____

Complete the Sentences Complete each sentence below.

6 One **fortuitous** occurrence was _____

7 It would **displease** me to _____

_____

8 I would like to **preserve** _____

9 If I had a **fortune**, I would _____

10 An **unfortunate** occurrence was _____

Speak It! Tell a partner about something that makes you happy or unhappy. Use several words from the Word List.

PART 3 Reference Skills

for Word Wisdom

Mind Over Matter:

Making Your Own Luck

Are some people really luckier than others? Can you make your own luck? Researchers have wondered about this for many years.

Richard Wiseman conducts research at a college in England. Wiseman decided to find out what makes some people lucky—or unlucky. Wiseman studied about 400 people. Some of these people considered themselves to be very lucky, while others thought of themselves as very unlucky. In his study, he discovered that people have more control over their lives than they think. In fact, Wiseman believes that we make our own luck.

Wiseman found that unlucky people like for things to stay the same. They are **annoyed** by new ideas. They want no part of them. But lucky people enjoy trying new things. They like to learn, explore, and make new friends. This increases their opportunities to experience good luck.

Unlucky people often have one goal, and they work hard to reach it. Their dedication is **noble**. However, when these people cannot reach their goal, they end up in **misery**.

In the meantime, they have ignored **precious** opportunities to find happiness. By thinking only about their goal, they have missed out on **marvelous** experiences.

Unlucky people also focus on what is wrong, not what is right. If an unlucky person has a car accident, he or she might say, "Look at my car! I can't believe my **horrific** luck!" After the same accident, a lucky person might say, "I am so glad that no one was badly hurt! Aren't we lucky?"

Lucky people face problems, but they aren't **tormented** by them. They look for something that is **favorable** about the experience. To them, nothing is that bad. They deal with the problem and know that things will get better.

Lucky people create their own opportunities. They do not wait for miracles. They do not expect any **charity** from others. They are relaxed about life and open to new experiences. They turn bad luck into good luck without even being aware of it. It seems that luck, good or bad, is a matter of attitude.

It's a **compliment** to be told you are lucky. Being lucky says good things about your approach to life. Maybe you are already a lucky person. If not, work on it!

Practice the Context Clues Strategy Here is one of the boldfaced words from the essay on page 172. Use the context clues strategy you learned in Part 1 on page 161 to figure out the meaning of this word.

annoyed

📖 **Read** the sentence that uses the word *annoyed* and some of the sentences around it.

🔍 **Look** for context clues to the word's meaning. What clues showing **How Something Is Done** can you find?

_____

_____

💡 **Think** about the context clues. What other helpful information do you know?

_____

_____

➡️ **Predict** a meaning for the word *annoy*.

_____

_____

_____

✔️ **Check** your Word Wisdom Dictionary to be sure of the meaning of the word *annoy*. Write the definition here.

_____

_____

_____

Unlock the Meanings

Part-of-Speech Labels Dictionary entries include part-of-speech labels for entry words. Some dictionaries use abbreviations for the parts of speech. Understanding these abbreviations can help you choose the correct form of a word to use in a sentence. Here are part-of-speech abbreviations you will find in dictionary entries.

n.—noun   **adv.**—adverb
pron.—pronoun   **prep.**—preposition
v.—verb   **interj.**—interjection
adj.—adjective   **conj.**—conjunction

Choose Parts of Speech Write the word that is the correct part of speech to complete each sentence. Then identify the part of speech by writing the correct abbreviation.

1 annoy *v.*   annoyance *n.*   annoying *adj.*

My brother's yelling was starting to ＿＿＿＿＿＿＿＿＿＿ me.

2 torment *v.*   torment *n.*   tormented *adj.*

He likes to ＿＿＿＿＿＿＿＿＿＿ me by teasing me until I cry.

3 noble *adj.*   nobly *adv.*   noble *n.*

The ＿＿＿＿＿＿＿＿＿＿ man ignored the rude comment.

4 compliment *n.*   complimented *v.*   compliment *v.*

I got a ＿＿＿＿＿＿＿＿＿＿ on my clean room.

5 favorable *adj.*   favorably *adv.*

He thought ＿＿＿＿＿＿＿＿＿＿ of the plan.

Find the Meaning

1. Use context clues.
2. Look for a familiar root, prefix, or suffix.
3. If the context or a word part doesn't help, check the dictionary.

Define the Words Follow the steps above to write the meaning of each boldfaced word. Then write 1, 2, or 3 to show which steps you used.

WORD LIST

annoy
noble
misery
precious
marvelous
horrific
torment
favorable
charity
compliment

1 Staying in a tent during a hurricane can bring **misery**.

_____

2 Mosquitoes that buzz around my head really **annoy** me.

_____

3 Our class had a bake sale to raise money for a **charity**.

_____

4 Don't **torment** me with loud noises.

_____

5 The flight was faster than usual because the wind was **favorable**.

_____

6 That double rainbow is **marvelous**.

_____

7 It's a **compliment** to be told I sing well.

_____

8 Some things are more **precious** than gold.

_____

9 It was **noble** of you to give your bus seat to another person.

_____

10 The sinking of the *Titanic* was a **horrific** accident.

_____

Process the Meanings

WORD LIST

annoy

noble

misery

precious

marvelous

horrific

torment

favorable

charity

compliment

Write the Missing Words Write the vocabulary word that contains the underlined word part and completes the sentence correctly.

1 Spring is my <u>fav</u>orite season since the weather is often

_____ for a picnic.

2 My sister <u>tor</u>tures me by humming in my ear, and I

_____ her by whistling for hours.

3 I feel <u>horr</u>ible, so I don't mind the _____ rain.

4 Jan and I called each other to say how <u>miser</u>able we felt; we

know that _____ loves company.

Rewrite the Sentences Rewrite each sentence using the word in parentheses.

5 The admirable firefighter got an award. (noble)

_____

6 Tim said my kick helped us win the game. (compliment)

_____

7 I gave food to a group that helps feed people. (charity)

_____

8 Bees may bother bears, but bears still get honey. (annoy)

_____

9 This scarf is special because my mom made it. (precious)

_____

10 You cooked the most wonderful dinner! (marvelous)

_____

Relate the Meanings Follow the directions or answer the questions.

1 Describe a person or an act that you consider **noble**.

_____

2 What **compliment** would you like someone to pay you?

_____

3 What kind of **charity** would you like to support?

_____

4 Describe something that is **precious** to you.

_____

5 Describe something that **annoys** you.

_____

6 Describe something that might cause a person **misery**.

_____

7 Describe something **marvelous** that happened to you.

_____

8 Describe how a dog might **torment** a cat.

_____

9 Describe some possible effects of a **horrific** storm.

_____

10 What time of year would be **favorable** for planting seeds outdoors?

_____

Write It! Describe the kindest act you have ever done or have ever seen. Use several words from the Word List.

Review

for Word Wisdom

WORD LIST

- conquer
- invade
- siege
- conserve
- determined
- desperate
- reassure
- misfortune
- astonish
- assume
- fortune
- preserve
- fortuitous
- pleasant
- unfortunate
- security
- displease
- pleasure
- deserve
- insecure
- annoy
- noble
- misery
- precious
- marvelous
- horrific
- torment
- favorable
- charity
- compliment

Sort by Connotation Say each word to yourself. Think about the feeling you get when you say each word. Is it good, bad, or neither? Write the word in the column you think it belongs in.

Good	Bad	Neither

Build Word Ladders Rearrange the vocabulary words within each group so that the words are in order from **best at the top** to **worst at the bottom.**

1 horrific _____

   pleasant _____

   marvelous _____

2 favorable _____

   precious _____

   desperate _____

3 displease _____

   compliment _____

   torment _____

4 preserve _____

   conquer _____

   invade _____

5 misfortune _____

   misery _____

   security _____

6 unfortunate _____

   fortuitous _____

   desperate _____

Demonstrate Word Knowledge Follow the directions.

7 Describe a time when you **deserved** something you received.

_____

8 Describe something that was a great **pleasure** for you.

_____

9 Describe what you might do if you had a **fortune**.

_____

10 Describe a time when you were **astonished**.

_____

11 Describe how a cat might act if someone **annoyed** it.

_____

Taking Vocabulary Tests

TEST-TAKING STRATEGY

Read the directions carefully whenever you take a test. Sometimes the directions change from one part of a test to another. For example, in one part of a vocabulary test, you may be asked to find synonyms. In another part of the test, you may need to find antonyms.

Sample A:

Fill in the letter of the answer choice that has the SAME or NEARLY THE SAME meaning as the underlined word.

good <u>publicity</u>

Ⓐ time
Ⓑ news
Ⓒ morning
Ⓓ party

Sample B:

Fill in the letter of the answer choice that has the OPPOSITE or NEARLY THE OPPOSITE meaning of the underlined word.

<u>complex</u> idea

Ⓐ new
Ⓑ worthy
Ⓒ simple
Ⓓ sudden

Practice Test For items 1–4, fill in the letter of the answer choice that has the SAME or NEARLY THE SAME meaning as the underlined word.

1 <u>precious</u> jewelry
Ⓐ worthless
Ⓑ pretty
Ⓒ valuable
Ⓓ personal

2 <u>astonish</u> me
Ⓐ accompany
Ⓑ surprise
Ⓒ offer
Ⓓ fool

3 <u>annoy</u> the neighbor
Ⓐ bother
Ⓑ visit
Ⓒ call
Ⓓ ignore

4 with <u>pleasure</u>
Ⓐ hunger
Ⓑ enjoyment
Ⓒ envy
Ⓓ anger

For items 5–10, fill in the letter of the answer choice that has the OPPOSITE or NEARLY THE OPPOSITE meaning of the underlined word.

5 <u>conserve</u> energy
Ⓐ save
Ⓑ burn
Ⓒ waste
Ⓓ find

6 <u>fortuitous</u> event
Ⓐ joyous
Ⓑ unlucky
Ⓒ recent
Ⓓ surprising

7 feeling of <u>misery</u>
Ⓐ calm
Ⓑ silliness
Ⓒ sadness
Ⓓ joy

8 <u>noble</u> gesture
Ⓐ unkind
Ⓑ generous
Ⓒ important
Ⓓ sudden

9 <u>preserve</u> photos
Ⓐ take
Ⓑ copy
Ⓒ display
Ⓓ discard

10 <u>invade</u> a country
Ⓐ discover
Ⓑ leave
Ⓒ take over
Ⓓ visit

Play with Language

Unscramble the Anagrams An **anagram** is a word puzzle. A word or a group of words is unscrambled to spell another word. Unscramble the anagrams below to form the correct words from the Word List on page 178.

1 vine ad _____

2 is not has _____

3 tune for tuna _____

4 ants leap _____

5 lip comment _____

6 same us _____

7 terms in deed _____

8 a lid seeps _____

Match Related Words Many words come from more than one language. Some of the words in this unit have Old French origins, as well as Latin roots. Match the words you know with other related words. Draw a line between each vocabulary word and its related word.

Old French Word	Vocabulary Word	Related Word
9 *charite*	charity	preservation
10 *preserver*	preserve	besieged
11 *sege*	siege	pleasantry
12 *plaisir*	pleasure	charitable

Speak It! Tell about a time when you had either good luck or bad luck. Use as many words from this unit as you can.

PART 1

Context Clues

for Word Wisdom

Working Together:

Building the Transcontinental Railroad

Imagine dangling from a rope and lighting sticks of dynamite. That was just one of the tasks performed by Chinese laborers who helped build the transcontinental railroad. Read more about the workers and the railroad.

In the 1800s, two companies started work on a railroad that would cross the whole United States, a transcontinental railroad. A railroad already existed from the East Coast to the Midwest. The Union Pacific Railroad began from a **locale** in Nebraska and moved west. The Central Pacific Railroad began from Sacramento, California, and moved east. Eventually, the two railroads would join.

Thousands of people had come from **provinces** in China to California. However, only a few Chinese workers were hired to work on the railroad. People did not understand their **foreign** customs. Some people did not **include** Chinese workers because they believed that the Chinese were not strong. Everything changed when one of the railroad owners remembered that the Chinese built the Great Wall of China. Eventually, many Chinese people were hired to work on the railroad.

Teams of workers laid **parallel** pieces of heavy metal rail with a tie to link them. Men labored twelve hours a day, six days a week. Chinese workers received an **approximate** rate of twenty-eight dollars a month, less than the other workers. Still, the Chinese teams were the best-organized and fastest workers.

The mountains of California were a major **obstacle** to laying railroad track. The solution was to blast through the rock. Small Chinese workers **descended** over a cliff from ropes. They cut holes in the rock and placed dynamite in the holes. Then the workers were hauled back up over the cliff before the dynamite exploded.

The two railroads finally met in May 1869. The **junction** was Promontory Point, Utah. Chinese workers helped to lay the last ten miles of track and helped pound in the very last spike. They made great **headway**, finishing in record time.

UNIT 9

Place and Position

Context Clues Strategy

Look for What Kind of Thing the Word Is

EXAMPLE: The powerful *locomotive* easily pulled the railroad cars over the track up the mountains.

CLUE: The words *powerful* and *easily pulled the railroad cars over the track* tell what kind of thing a *locomotive* is.

Here are steps for using this context clues strategy to figure out the meaning of the word *obstacle*, from page 182.

Read the sentence with the unknown word and some of the sentences around it.

* * * * *

*The mountains of California were a major **obstacle** to laying railroad track. The solution was to blast through the rock.*

Look for context clues. What clues showing **What Kind of Thing the Word Is** can you find?

* * * * *

Workers had to blast through the rock. An *obstacle* may be something that is in the way.

Think about the context clues and other helpful information you know.

* * * * *

An *obstacle* race has things blocking a runner's way.

Predict a meaning for the word.

* * * * *

The word *obstacle* must mean "something that gets in the way of doing something."

Check a dictionary to be sure of the meaning.

* * * * *

An *obstacle* is "something in the way."

Unlock the Meanings

Practice the Strategy   Here is one of the boldfaced words from the article on page 182. Use the context clues strategy on page 183 to figure out the meaning of the word.

locale

Read the sentence that uses the word *locale* and some of the sentences around it.

Look for context clues. What clues showing **What Kind of Thing the Word Is** can you find?

_____

_____

_____

Think about the context clues. What other helpful information do you know?

_____

_____

_____

Predict a meaning for the word.

_____

_____

_____

Check your Word Wisdom Dictionary to be sure of the meaning of the word *locale*. Write the dictionary meaning.

_____

_____

Use Context Clues You have been introduced to two of the boldfaced words from the article on page 182. These words are checked off in the Word List. In the first column, write the other eight words from the Word List. In the second column, predict a meaning for each word. Then look up the meaning in a dictionary. In the third column, write the dictionary meaning that fits the context.

WORD LIST

✔ locale
province
foreign
include
parallel
approximate
✔ obstacle
descend
junction
headway

Vocabulary Word	Your Prediction	Dictionary Says
1		
2		
3		
4		
5		
6		
7		
8		

Process the Meanings

WORD LIST

locale

province

foreign

include

parallel

approximate

obstacle

descend

junction

headway

Complete the Sentences Write the best word from the Word List to complete each sentence.

1 Be sure not to trip on any _____ in the hallway.

2 A _____ has many things in common with a county or a state.

3 The beach is a wonderful _____ for resting or playing.

4 The two tracks of a railroad run _____ to each other.

5 Be sure to _____ the author's name when you write your book report.

Complete the Analogies Choose the best word from each pair in parentheses to complete the analogy. Write your answer on the line.

6 Stillness is to silence as progress is to (obstacle, headway).

_____

7 Finish is to ending as connection is to (junction, locale).

_____

8 Inside is to outside as climb is to (descend, include).

_____

9 At home is to familiar as away is to (foreign, obstacle).

_____

10 Clear is to blurry as exact is to (parallel, approximate).

_____

Demonstrate Word Knowledge Use what you've learned about the boldfaced words to answer the questions or follow the directions.

1 Which **foreign** country would you like to visit? Why?

_____

2 Name a **province** in Canada or another country.

_____

3 Describe a time when you had trouble making **headway**.

_____

4 Describe two things you can see that are **parallel**.

_____

5 What is the **approximate** length of your hand in inches?

_____

6 Describe a time when you felt **included** in a special event.

_____

7 Describe the **locale** of one of your favorite books or movies.

_____

8 What might you see if you **descend** deep into the ocean?

_____

9 Name someone who overcame an **obstacle**.

_____

10 Describe a **junction** that is near your school.

_____

Write It! Write about a trip that you took. Use as many words from the Word List in Part 1 as you can.

PART 2

Latin Roots

for Word Wisdom

Protecting Wildlife:
Habitat Hallways

Every day, the territory of humans grows—our green land is turned into urban space, and our cities and roads expand. But what happens to the wildlife that once lived in these areas?

Wild salmon migrate throughout their lives. Most salmon leave the ocean to lay eggs in rivers and streams. After they hatch, baby salmon swim to the ocean where they grow. After time, they return to their home river or stream. Today many dams block rivers. They prevent the salmon from migrating and laying their eggs. Some kinds of wild salmon may soon be extinct.

The Alaskan caribou is another animal that must move from one area to another. Their range gets very cold in winter. They must migrate south to find food. Some herds travel a **distance** of 400 miles. On this trip, they must have enough space to find food and to outrun their predators. However, roads, oil pipelines, and oil pumping **stations** now cross this land. These structures can get in the way of the caribou's **relocation**.

Many wild habitats are now **enclosed** by towns and cities. They are surrounded by ranches and **estates**. Some areas are fenced in. These fences **exclude** people from these habitats. They also prevent the animals from migrating. When wild things cannot migrate, they suffer. They have fewer babies. They are not as healthy. On the other hand, healthy groups of animals have many babies. Then the **local** habitat becomes too small to support them. Some members must move to a new area.

One solution is wildlife corridors. These corridors are like hallways that connect wildlife areas. They allow animals to migrate in a natural way. Some groups are working to protect wildlife corridors from human development. They have taken the **stance** that wildlife should not be **dislocated** from its habitats. They know that the **closure** of a corridor can mean death for some animals. The predators that hunt them will be the next to suffer. In time, the entire food chain can be affected.

The animals that need these corridors range from salamanders to grizzly bears. We must work together to protect them.

Practice the Context Clues Strategy Here is one of the boldfaced words from the essay on page 188. Use the context clues strategy you learned in Part 1 on page 183 to figure out the meaning of this word.

distance

📖 **Read** the sentence that uses the word *distance* and some of the sentences around it.

🔍 **Look** for context clues to the word's meaning. What clues showing **What Kind of Thing the Word Is** can you find?

_____

_____

_____

💡 **Think** about the context clues. What other helpful information do you know?

_____

_____

_____

➡️ **Predict** a meaning for the word *distance*.

_____

_____

_____

✔️ **Check** your Word Wisdom Dictionary to be sure of the meaning of the word *distance*. Which of the meanings for the word fits the context?

_____

_____

_____

Many words you use come from Latin roots. Knowing the meanings of different roots can help you figure out the meaning of new words. Several words you learned in Part 1 have a Latin root. Each root relates to place or position.

Latin Root: **clu, clo, clud**
meaning: to close; to shut
English word: *include*
meaning: to close in as part of

Latin Root: **sta**
meaning: to stand
English word: *obstacle*
meaning: difficulty; barrier

Latin Root: **loc**
meaning: a place
English word: *locale*
meaning: a setting

WORD LIST

distance
station
relocation
enclose
estate
exclude
local
stance
dislocate
closure

Sort by Roots Find these roots in the Word List. Write each word under the correct root. Think of other words that come from the same Latin roots. Write each word under the correct root.

Latin Root: clu, clo, clud	Latin Root: sta	Latin Root: loc

Place and Position

Prefix	Meaning	Example
en-	in, into	

en- (in) + **clo** (to close) + **se** = **enclose**

Use Roots and Prefixes Circle the root and any prefix you find in the boldfaced words. Use context clues, roots, and prefixes to write the meaning of each word. Check your definitions in a dictionary.

1 My mom's new job in another state requires our **relocation**.

_____

2 She will manage a large **estate**.

_____

3 The governor announced the **closure** of state parks during the dry spell.

_____

4 Forest fires may **dislocate** people and animals that live nearby.

_____

5 We could tell he was an athlete by his upright and confident **stance**.

_____

6 Some firefighters are **local** people; others come from farther away.

_____

7 If you try to **exclude** your brother from your room, do you succeed?

_____

8 You may pay for your purchase inside the gas **station**.

_____

9 The fires spread a great **distance** through the mountains.

_____

10 A playpen is one way to **enclose** babies so they don't get hurt.

_____

WORD LIST

distance
station
relocation
enclose
estate
exclude
local
stance
dislocate
closure

Replace the Words   After each sentence, write the word from the Word List that can replace the underlined words.

1 Do you know who lives on the large property behind that wall? _____

2 Have you ever traveled a long way from your home?

_____

3 Randy tried not to make anyone feel unwelcome when planning his party. _____

4 My aunt helps in finding homes in new places for people in her company. _____

5 Maybe someone in that place that provides a service can give us directions. _____

Use Context Clues   Write the word from the Word List that best completes each sentence.

6 What is your _____ on the topic?

7 Our neighbors decided to _____ their porch to make an extra room.

8 If you ever _____ your shoulder, you will discover that it is very painful.

9 Listen to the radio for announcements about the

_____ of schools because of snowstorms.

10 Is there a good _____ restaurant nearby?

Link to Your Life Respond to each question or statement.

1 Describe a favorite **local** place to meet others. _____

_____

2 Tell about a time you traveled a long **distance**. _____

_____

3 Describe an **estate** that you have read about or visited. _____

_____

4 Describe a type of **station** that you have been to. _____

_____

5 How would someone describe your **stance**? _____

_____

Demonstrate Word Knowledge Complete each statement.

6 A group that might **exclude** people based on age is _____

_____

7 Someone who can help others with **relocation** is _____

_____

8 Wild animals may be **dislocated** by _____

9 Something that might cause a **closure** of a place is _____

_____

10 Something that may be **enclosed** is _____

_____

 Speak It! Tell a classmate about a place you once visited. Use as many Part 2 words as you can.

Reference Skills

for Word Wisdom

City or Country?

Choosing a College

Have you thought about going to college yet? Do you have a certain college in mind? Choosing a college is a difficult decision. Should you go to a large college or a small one? Should you choose a college in a city or out in the country?

A college **campus** in the country offers many benefits. Living on a **rural** campus means having more room. It also means less air pollution and fewer tall buildings. Your walk to classes might take you past towering trees and across green lawns. You would probably live in a **dormitory** and get to know many other students who live there. If the college is in a farming **region,** the nearest town might be miles away, so you would spend most of your time on the campus. You might belong to several groups or clubs. You might also play on a dorm or college sports team.

Many **urban** colleges have high-rise classroom buildings and laboratory **facilities**. If the college is in the **interior** of the city, you might walk to classes through busy streets. You might have to ride a bus or a

subway. Younger students often live in dormitories with many floors and small **chambers**. Older students are likely to live in apartments off campus. In a city college, you would spend more of your time off campus. For entertainment, you would have a wide choice of restaurants and theaters. You might be able to eat food and hear music from all over the world. These attractions, however, can become distractions. They might make it harder to pay attention to your studies.

You could compromise. Consider a college set on the **fringe** of a large city. Far from being on the **frontier** of civilization, this college would offer more room than an urban school. It also would offer more activities than a rural school. A short bus ride would take you to stores and restaurants. Still, you would live far enough away from these distractions to focus on your classwork.

Choosing a college is not easy. Study hard now and keep your grades up. Then you will have many choices for college when the time comes. You can decide for yourself whether to go to school in the city or in the country.

Practice the Context Clues Strategy Here is one of the boldfaced words from the essay on page 194. Use the context clues strategy you learned in Part 1 on page 183 to figure out the meaning of this word.

dormitory

Read the sentence that uses the word *dormitory* and some of the sentences around it.

Look for context clues to the word's meaning. What clues showing **What Kind of Thing the Word Is** can you find?

_____

_____

_____

Think about the context clues. What other helpful information do you know?

_____

_____

_____

Predict a meaning for the word *dormitory*.

_____

_____

_____

Check your Word Wisdom Dictionary to be sure of the meaning of the word *dormitory*. Write the definition here.

_____

_____

_____

Multiple Meanings Some words have more than one meaning. Many dictionaries include all the meanings in one entry and number them. Look at this dictionary entry for the word *chamber*.

> **cham•ber** /chām′ bər/ *n.* **1.** a bedroom or other room in a house or apartment. **2.** a room in a palace. **3.** a meeting hall for a governing body. **4.** an organization formed for a special purpose. **5.** a compartment or small space, such as a chamber of the heart.

Choose the Meanings Use the dictionary entry above. Read each sentence below, and decide which meaning of the word *chamber* fits the context of the sentence. Write the number on the line.

1 The queen met with her advisers in her **chamber**. _____

2 Many cities have a **chamber** of commerce, which helps local businesses. _____

3 The U.S. Senate meets in one **chamber**, and the House of Representatives meets in another. _____

4 The human heart has four sections, called **chambers**, which let blood in and out. _____

5 My piano teacher calls her living room "the music **chamber**" because she uses that room only for teaching and performing music. _____

6 The attorneys discussed the trial in the judge's **chambers**. _____

Find the Meaning

1. Use context clues.
2. Look for a familiar root, prefix, or suffix.
3. If the context or a word part doesn't help, check the dictionary.

Define the Words Follow the steps above to write the meaning of each boldfaced word. Write 1, 2, or 3 to show which steps you used.

WORD LIST

campus
rural
dormitory
region
urban
facility
interior
chamber
fringe
frontier

1 Many college students live in a **dormitory**.

_____

2 The snail pulled back into the **interior** of its shell.

_____

3 Trees were planted on the **fringe** of the street.

_____

4 Fewer people live in **rural** areas than in cities.

_____

5 Who were the people who settled the Western **frontier**?

_____

6 The **chamber** is in the center of the building.

_____

7 My brother mows the grass on the **campus** of the private school.

_____

8 That **facility** is used for medical research.

_____

9 Winters are cold in the northeast **region** of the United States.

_____

10 People who design cities are called **urban** planners.

_____

WORD LIST

- campus
- rural
- dormitory
- region
- urban
- facility
- interior
- chamber
- fringe
- frontier

Rewrite the Sentences Rewrite each sentence using the vocabulary word in parentheses.

1 My brother stays in a place where students live. (dormitory)

_____

2 Iowa is a state in the inner part of the United States. (interior)

_____

3 The fire station is on the edge of the small town. (fringe)

_____

4 The college property has many buildings. (campus)

_____

5 My mother grew up in a city neighborhood in Chicago. (urban)

_____

6 Raj is from a small village in the countryside in India. (rural)

_____

7 The meeting took place in a large room. (chamber)

_____

8 As the United States grew, the undeveloped area moved west. (frontier)

_____

9 My great-aunt lives in that retirement home. (facility)

_____

10 That area of Arizona has lots of mountains. (region)

_____

Relate the Meanings Use what you've learned about the boldfaced words to follow the directions or answer the questions.

1 What is a large **facility** in your city or town? _____

_____

2 What does it mean if a scientist is on the **frontier** of research?

_____

3 Describe what can be found in the **interior** of your closet. _____

_____

4 In college, would you like to live in a **dormitory**? Explain.

_____

5 Describe an **urban** area you would like to visit. _____

_____

6 Explain whether your school has a **campus**. _____

_____

7 Describe what is on the **fringe** of your city or town. _____

_____

8 Name two places in which you could find a **chamber**. _____

_____

9 Describe a **rural** place you would like to visit. _____

_____

10 In which **region** of the United States do you live? _____

_____

Write It! Describe a building or an area that is important to you. Use as many words from the Word List in Part 3 as you can.

PART
4

Review

for Word Wisdom

Sort the Words by Meaning Sort the words in the Word List by Words That Name Places, Words That Describe Places, and Other Words. Write each word in the correct column of the chart.

WORD LIST

locale
province
foreign
include
parallel
approximate
obstacle
descend
junction
headway
distance
station
relocation
enclose
estate
exclude
local
stance
dislocate
closure
campus
rural
dormitory
region
urban
facility
interior
chamber
fringe
frontier

Words That Name Places	Words That Describe Places	Other Words

Review

Connect the Meanings Write a sentence that uses the vocabulary words in each group in any order. You may add endings to the words.

1 obstacle, dislocate _____

2 distance, rural _____

3 province, foreign, estate _____

4 chamber, interior, relocation _____

5 facility, dormitory, campus _____

Demonstrate Word Knowledge Answer the questions.

6 What is the **approximate** travel time from your school to the **fringe** of your yard?

7 Can you name something in the room that is **parallel**?

8 What's your **stance** on drinking soda with every meal?

9 What kind of **obstacle** might lead to the **closure** of a road?

10 What might you find at the **junction** of two streets?

Taking Vocabulary Tests

✏ TEST-TAKING STRATEGY

On a vocabulary test, try to answer the questions before you look at the answer choices. Then see if one of the choices is close to what you guessed. When you finish the test, go back over your answers. Make sure you did not skip any items. Do not change any answers unless you are certain that your first choice was incorrect. If the directions tell you to fill in circles, as this test does, be sure you fill them in completely.

Sample:

Fill in the circle for the word that has the same or nearly the same meaning as the boldfaced word.

locale
- O bird
- O idea
- ◉ place
- O neighbor

Practice Test Fill in the circle of the answer choice that has the SAME or NEARLY THE SAME meaning as the boldfaced word.

1 exclude
- O keep out
- O gather up
- O permit
- O invite

2 descend
- O whisper
- O move up
- O yell
- O move down

3 rural
- O country
- O starry
- O city
- O cloudy

4 enclose
- O enter
- O melt
- O surround
- O open

5 region
- O state
- O town
- O country
- O area

6 frontier
- O moon
- O border
- O river
- O railroad

7 urban
- O helmet
- O city
- O ruler
- O busy

8 obstacle
- O barrier
- O mountain
- O rock
- O planet

9 interior
- O shell
- O house
- O inside
- O front

10 headway
- O headlong
- O origin
- O progress
- O problem

Build New Words

Make Word Webs You can make many new words from the vocabulary words *station* and *local*. Add the letters shown below to make new words.

station

Add: -ery
Meaning: writing paper

New Word: _____

Add: -ed
Meaning: assigned to a place

New Word: _____

Add: -ary
Meaning: not moving

New Word: _____

local

Add: -ity
Meaning: a neighborhood

New Word: _____

Add: -ize
Meaning: to restrict to a certain area

New Word: _____

Add: -ism
Meaning: the custom of a certain area

New Word: _____

Speak It! What kind of locale do you live in—a city, a rural area, or something in between? Describe it. What's special about your locale? What would you like to change about it? Use as many words from this Place and Position unit as you can.

WORD Wisdom Dictionary

PRONUNCIATION KEY	
/ă/	pat
/ā/	pay
/â/	care
/ä/	father
/är/	far
/ĕ/	pet
/ē/	be
/ĭ/	pit
/ī/	pie
/îr/	pier
/ŏ/	mop
/ō/	toe
/ô/	paw, for
/oi/	noise
/ou/	out
/ŏŏ/	look
/ōō/	boot
/ŭ/	cut
/ûr/	urge
/th/	thin
/th/	this
/hw/	what
/zh/	vision
/ə/	about
	item
	pencil
	gallop
	circus
/ər/	butter

A

ab•stract¹ /ăb străkt′ *or* ăb′ străkt′/ *adj.* not easily understood. *His abstract ideas left us confused and unsure.* —**ab•stract•ly** *adv.* —**ab•stract•ness** *n.*

ab•stract² /ăb străkt′ *or* ăb′ străkt′/ *adj.* consisting of designs or shapes that are not realistic forms. *We enjoyed the abstract art at the museum.* —**ab•stract•ly** *adv.* —**ab•stract•ness** *n.*

ab•stract³ /ăb străkt′/ *v.* **ab•stract•ed, ab•stract•ing, ab•stracts.** to take away; to remove. *In this experiment, we will abstract the fat from the cheese.*

ac•com•pa•ny /ə kŭm′ pə nē *or* ə kŭmp′ nē/ *v.* **ac•com•pa•nied, ac•com•pa•ny•ing, ac•com•pa•nies.** to go with. *I will accompany my brother to the airport.*

ad•mi•ra•ble /ăd′ mər ə bəl/ *adj.* worthy of respect. *Her honesty was admirable.* —**ad•mi•ra•bly** *adv.*

ad•vance¹ /ăd văns′/ *v.* **ad•vanced, ad•vanc•ing, ad•vanc•es.** to move forward or move ahead. *She advanced to second place in the contest.*

ad•vance² /ăd văns′/ *v.* **ad•vanced, ad•vanc•ing, ad•vanc•es.** to pay ahead; to pay something before it is due. *Dad advanced my allowance so I could go to the movie.*

ad•vance³ /ăd văns′/ *n.* a payment ahead of time. *We gave the builder an advance to start work on the house.*

ad•ven•tur•ous /ăd vĕn′ chər əs/ *adj.* seeking new experience; willing to take risks; bold. *An adventurous group climbed the mountain.* —**ad•ven•tur•ous•ly** *adv.* —**ad•ven•tur•ous•ness** *n.*

af•fec•tion /ə fĕk′ shən/ *n.* a tenderness felt for someone or something. *The child showed great affection for her doll.*

a•gree•a•ble¹ /ə grē′ ə bəl/ *adj.* pleasing; pleasant. *Her agreeable personality won us over.* —**a•gree•a•bly** *adv.* —**a•gree•a•ble•ness** *n.*

a•gree•a•ble² /ə grē′ ə bəl/ *adj.* ready to agree or consent. *I was agreeable to the picnic plans.* —**a•gree•a•bly** *adv.* —**a•gree•a•ble•ness** *n.*

an•noy /ə noi′/ *v.* **an•noyed, an•noy•ing, an•noys.** to bother; to irritate. *Gnats annoy me.*

anx•ious¹ /ăngk′ shəs *or* ăng′ shəs/ *adj.* worried; uneasy. *We became anxious when our dog didn't return immediately.* —**anx•ious•ly** *adv.* —**anx•ious•ness** *n.*

anx•ious² /ăngk′ shəs *or* ăng′ shəs/ *adj.* eagerly wishing. *They were anxious for the party to begin.* —**anx•ious•ly** *adv.* —**anx•ious•ness** *n.*

ap•par•ent¹ /ə păr′ ənt *or* ə pâr′ ənt/ *adj.* easily seen; evident. *The stain on the white shirt was quite apparent.* —**ap•par•ent•ly** *adv.* —**ap•par•ent•ness** *n.*

ap•par•ent² /ə păr′ ənt *or* ə pâr′ ənt/ *adj.* plainly understood; obvious. *It was apparent that they didn't understand the lesson.* —**ap•par•ent•ly** *adv.* —**ap•par•ent•ness** *n.*

ap•pa•ri•tion /ăp′ ə rĭsh′ ən/ *n.* a ghostly-looking image. *An apparition appeared in the dark window.*

ap•pear•ance¹ /ə pîr′ əns/ *n.* the way a person looks to himself or herself or others. *The new hairstyle changed my appearance.*

ap•pear•ance² /ə pîr′ əns/ *n.* the act of coming into view. *His sudden appearance startled me.*

ap•pear•ance³ /ə pîr′ əns/ *n.* a false show. *The outraged customer put on a calm appearance.*

ap•pro•pri•ate¹ /ə prō′ prē ĭt/ *adj.* suitable or proper. *Heavy clothing will be appropriate for the northern trip.* —**ap•pro•pri•ate•ly** *adv.* —**ap•pro•pri•ate•ness** *n.*

ap•pro•pri•ate² /ə prō′ prē āt/ *v.* **ap•pro•pri•at•ed, ap•pro•pri•at•ing, ap•pro•pri•ates.** to set apart or take. *The school district appropriated money for new books.* —**ap•pro•pri•a•tive** *adj.* —**ap•pro•pri•a•tor** *n.*

ap•prox•i•mate¹ /ə prŏk′ sə mĭt/ *adj.* almost exact. *The approximate time of our arrival was noon.* —**ap•prox•i•mate•ly** *adv.*

ap•prox•i•mate² /ə prŏk′ sə māt/ *v.* **ap•prox•i•mat•ed, ap•prox•i•mat•ing, ap•prox•i•mates.** to come close; to be nearly the same as. *The seating in the theater approximates two hundred.* —**ap•prox•i•mate•ly** *adv.*

aq•ua•ma•rine¹ /ăk′ wə mə rēn′ *or* ä′ kwə mə rēn′/ *n.* a pale blue-green color. *The water in the pool is aquamarine.*

aq•ua•ma•rine² /ăk′ wə mə rēn′ *or* ä′ kwə mə rēn′/ *n.* a pale blue-green gemstone. *Aquamarine is the March birthstone.*

a•quar•i•um /ə kwâr′ ē əm/ *n., pl.* **a•quar•i•ums** *or* **a•quar•i•a** /ə kwâr′ ē ə/ a container of water for fish, animals, or plants. *Our classroom aquarium is filled with goldfish.*

a•quat•ic /ə kwăt′ ĭk *or* ə kwŏt′ ĭk/ *adj.* relating to water. *Aquatic plants are food for many fish.*

aq•ue•duct /ăk′ wĭ dŭkt′/ *n.* a pipe for carrying water. *The Romans built aqueducts to their cities.*

ar•chae•ol•o•gist *or* **ar•che•ol•o•gist** /är′ kē ŏl′ ə jĭst/ *n.* a person who studies remains of objects from the past, such as tools and pottery. *My brother wants to be an archaeologist.*

a•shamed /ə shāmd′/ *adj.* feeling shame. *I felt ashamed for lying.* —**a•sham•ed•ly** /ə shā′ mĭd lē/ *adv.*

as•so•ci•a•tion /ə sō′ sē ā′ shən *or* ə sō′ shē ā′ shən/ *n.* a group of people with the same interests. *The parent association will meet to plan the school picnic.* —**as•so•ci•a•tion•al** *adj.*

as•sume /ə so͞om′/ *v.* **as•sumed, as•sum•ing, as•sumes.** to suppose. *I assume the plane will leave on time.* —**as•sum•a•ble** *adj.* —**as•sum•a•bly** *adv.* —**as•sum•er** *n.*

as•ter•oid /ăs′ tə roid′/ *n.* a large chunk of rock orbiting the sun. *We looked through a telescope to see the asteroid.*

a•ston•ish /ə stŏn′ ĭsh/ *v.* **a•ston•ished, a•ston•ish•ing, a•ston•ish•es.** to surprise or amaze. *I was astonished to win the contest.* —**a•ston•ish•ing•ly** *adv.*

as•tro•naut /ăs′ trə nôt′/ *n.* a person who is trained to serve on a spacecraft. *An astronaut wears special clothes in space.*

as•tron•o•my /ə strŏn′ ə mē/ *n., pl.* **as•tron•o•mies.** the study of stars and planets. *In my book about astronomy, I read about the Milky Way.*

at•mos•phere /ăt′ mə sfîr′/ *n.* the gases and air that surround our planet or other heavenly bodies. *Earth's atmosphere affects the weather.*

B

bac•te•ri•a /băk tîr′ ē ə/ *n., pl. of* **bac•te•ri•um** /băk tîr′ ē əm/ tiny, one-celled organisms, some of which can cause disease. *The harmful bacteria caused the child to become quite ill.*

bar•ri•er /băr′ ē ər/ *n.* something that blocks something else. *A barrier was placed at the entrance of the street.*

bil•low /bĭl′ ō/ *v.* **bil•lowed, bil•low•ing, bil•lows.** to surge; to wave. *The curtains billowed in the wind.* —**bil•low•y** *adj.* —**bil•low•i•ness** *n.*

bolt¹ /bōlt/ *n.* a threaded pin or rod used to hold things together. *We used bolts to put the boards together.*

bolt² /bōlt/ *n.* a rod; a sliding bar used for fastening. *Latch the bolt on the gate as you leave.*

bolt³ /bōlt/ *v.* **bolt•ed, bolt•ing, bolts.** to fasten with a bolt. *She bolted the baby swing to the floor so it wouldn't tip over.*

bolt⁴ /bōlt/ *v.* **bolt•ed, bolt•ing, bolts.** to move suddenly; to run away. *The horse bolted when the gate was opened.*

C

cam•pus /kăm′ pəs/ *n., pl.* **cam•pus•es.** the grounds of a school or other institution. *I met my friend at the fountain on campus.*

can•ter /kăn′ tər/ *v.* **can•tered, can•ter•ing, can•ters.** to move at a slow, casual pace or gallop. *The horses cantered across the meadow.*

cav•ern /kăv′ ərn/ *n.* a very large cave. *We found many bats in the dark cavern.*

cav•i•ty¹ /kăv′ ĭ tē/ *n., pl.* **cav•i•ties.** a hole or hollow area. *The constant rainfall caused a small cavity in the soft stone.*

cav•i•ty² /kăv′ ĭ tē/ *n., pl.* **cav•i•ties.** an area of decay in a tooth. *The dentist said I had one new cavity.*

cham•ber¹ /chām′ bər/ *n.* a room. *The bedroom chambers of the castle were small.*

cham•ber² /chām′ bər/ *n.* an enclosed space. *A small chamber near the back of the cave stayed warm and dry.*

char•i•ty¹ /chăr′ ĭ tē/ *n., pl.* **char•i•ties.** a fund or organization for helping the needy. *We will give money to a charity.*

char•i•ty² /chăr′ ĭ tē/ *n., pl.* **char•i•ties.** goodwill toward others; a generous act. *Helping the blind woman to cross the street was an act of charity.*

clar•i•ty /klăr′ ĭ tē/ *n.* the state or quality of being clear. *He explained the answer with clarity.*

clo•sure /klō′ zhər/ *n.* the act of closing or shutting down. *The closure of the highway caused a major traffic jam.*

com•pas•sion•ate /kəm păsh′ ə nĭt/ *adj.* feeling sympathy or compassion. *The nurse's compassionate care comforted the sick woman.* —**com•pas•sion•ate•ly** *adv.*

com•pat•i•ble /kəm păt′ ə bəl/ *adj.* in agreement; able to work together. *The teacher and his students seemed compatible.* —**com•pat•i•bly** *adv.* —**com•pat•i•bil•i•ty** *n.*

com•pli•ment¹ /kŏm′ plə mənt/ *n.* an expression of praise or admiration. *It was a compliment to be asked to speak at the meeting.*

com•pli•ment² /kŏm′ plə mənt/ *v.* **com•pli•ment•ed, com•pli•ment•ing, com•pli•ments.** to praise. *The teacher complimented the students on their hard work.*

com•pro•mise¹ /kŏm′ prə mīz′/ *n.* an agreement in which each side gives up a little. *The committee reached a compromise that made everyone happy.*

com•pro•mise² /kŏm′ prə mīz′/ *v.* **com•pro•mised, com•pro•mis•ing, com•pro•mis•es.** to settle a disagreement with a compromise. *I compromised and agreed to order veggie pizza instead of pepperoni.* —**com•pro•mis•er** *n.*

PRONUNCIATION KEY	
/ă/	pat
/ā/	pay
/â/	care
/ä/	father
/är/	far
/ĕ/	pet
/ē/	be
/ĭ/	pit
/ī/	pie
/îr/	pier
/ŏ/	mop
/ō/	toe
/ô/	paw, for
/oi/	noise
/ou/	out
/o͝o/	look
/o͞o/	boot
/ŭ/	cut
/ûr/	urge
/th/	thin
/th/	this
/hw/	what
/zh/	vision
/ə/	about
	item
	pencil
	gallop
	circus
/ər/	butter

con•duct¹ /kən dŭkt′/ v. **con•duct•ed, con•duct•ing, con•ducts.** to lead or direct. *A volunteer conducted a tour through the museum.* —**con•duct•i•ble** adj. —**con•duct•i•bil•i•ty** n.

con•duct² /kən dŭkt′/ v. **con•duct•ed, con•duct•ing, con•ducts.** to act in a certain way. *The children conducted themselves well during the play.* —**con•duct•i•ble** adj. —**con•duct•i•bil•i•ty** n.

con•fess /kən fĕs′/ v. **con•fessed, con•fess•ing, con•fess•es.** to admit a fault or deed. *Dad confessed that he had eaten the last cookie.*

con•fi•dent /kŏn′ fĭ dənt/ adj. sure of oneself. *He felt confident about his test performance.* —**con•fi•dent•ly** adv.

con•gre•gate /kŏng′ grĭ gāt′/ v. **con•gre•gat•ed, con•gre•gat•ing, con•gre•gates.** to gather together. *The children like to congregate in the toy area.* —**con•gre•ga•tive** adj. —**con•gre•ga•tor** n.

con•quer /kŏng′ kər/ v. **con•quered, con•quer•ing, con•quers.** to defeat. *The swimmer conquered her fear of diving.* —**con•quer•a•ble** adj. —**con•quer•or** or **con•quer•er** n.

con•serve /kən sûrv′/ v. **con•served, con•serv•ing, con•serves.** to use carefully and without wasting. *We must conserve our water supply.* —**con•serv•a•ble** adj. —**con•serv•er** n.

con•sid•er•ate /kən sĭd′ ər ĭt/ adj. thoughtful; having regard for others' needs and feelings. *Our school nurse is considerate of our comfort.* —**con•sid•er•ate•ly** adv. —**con•sid•er•ate•ness** n.

con•ta•gious /kən tā′ jəs/ adj. able to be spread to others. *The flu is highly contagious.* —**con•ta•gious•ly** adv. —**con•ta•gious•ness** n.

cor•rect¹ /kə rĕkt′/ v. **cor•rect•ed, cor•rect•ing, cor•rects.** to remove mistakes from. *The teacher had us correct our math tests.* —**cor•rect•ly** adv. —**cor•rect•ness** n.

cor•rect² /kə rĕkt′/ adj. accurate. *You have the correct answers.*

cour•te•ous /kûr′ tē əs/ adj. being polite and considerate. *The store clerk was courteous to the customers.* —**cour•te•ous•ly** adv. —**cour•te•ous•ness** n.

crank•y /krăng′ kē/ adj. **crank•i•er, crank•i•est.** cross; complaining. *He was cranky because he was tired.* —**crank•i•ly** adv. —**crank•i•ness** n.

cra•ter /krā′ tər/ n. a bowl-shaped hole in the earth. *The meteorite formed a crater in the earth.*

cun•ning /kŭn′ ĭng/ adj. sly; skilled at cheating or tricking. *The thief's cunning ways kept the police from catching him.* —**cun•ning•ly** adv.

cu•ri•ous /kyŏŏr′ ē əs/ adj. interested; eager to know more. *The child was curious about where the ants were going.* —**cu•ri•ous•ly** adv. —**cu•ri•ous•ness** n.

cus•tom /kŭs′ təm/ n. the habits of a particular group of people. *It is our family's custom to go out to eat for birthdays.*

D

dec•o•rate /dĕk′ ə rāt′/ v. **dec•o•rat•ed, dec•o•rat•ing, dec•o•rates.** to furnish with something attractive; to make attractive. *The children decorated the cookies with frosting.*

dec•o•ra•tive /dĕk′ ər ə tĭv or dĕk′ ə rā′ tĭv/ adj. ornamental. *She bought several decorative pillows for her couch.* —**dec•o•ra•tive•ly** adv.

de•fect¹ /dē′ fĕkt′ or dĭ fĕkt′/ n. an imperfection. *The beautiful new bike had a defect.*

de•fect² /dĭ fĕkt′/ v. **de•fect•ed, de•fect•ing, de•fects.** to leave without permission; to desert. *The visiting athlete defected and refused to return to her native country.* —**de•fec•tor** n.

de•form /dĭ fôrm′/ v. **de•formed, de•form•ing, de•forms.** to misshape; to spoil the form or shape of. *Burning the candles will deform them.* —**de•form•a•ble** adj.

de•formed /dĭ fôrmd′/ adj. misshapen. *The dog's deformed leg made it difficult for him to run.*

dem•on•strate /dĕm′ ən strāt′/ v. **dem•on•strat•ed, dem•on•strat•ing, dem•on•strates.** to explain or show how to do something. *The teacher will demonstrate the correct way to work the math problem.*

dense /dĕns/ adj. **dens•er, dens•est.** crowded; thick. *The dense ivy covered the brick wall.* —**dense•ly** adv. —**dense•ness** n.

**PRONUNCIATION
KEY**

/ă/	pat
/ā/	pay
/â/	care
/ä/	father
/är/	far
/ĕ/	pet
/ē/	be
/ĭ/	pit
/ī/	pie
/îr/	pier
/ŏ/	mop
/ō/	toe
/ô/	paw, for
/oi/	noise
/ou/	out
/o͝o/	look
/o͞o/	boot
/ŭ/	cut
/ûr/	urge
/th/	thin
/th/	this
/hw/	what
/zh/	vision
/ə/	about
	item
	pencil
	gallop
	circus
/ər/	butter

de•scend /dĭ sĕnd′/ v. **de•scend•ed, de•scend•ing, de•scends.** to move down. *The plane descended through the clouds.*

de•serve /dĭ zûrv′/ v. **de•served, de•serv•ing, de•serves.** to be worthy of. *He deserves an award for his good work.*

des•per•ate¹ /dĕs′ pər ĭt/ adj. nearly hopeless; showing despair. *The lost hikers were in a desperate situation.* —**des•per•ate•ly** adv. —**des•per•ate•ness** n.

des•per•ate² /dĕs′ pər ĭt/ adj. reckless because of urgency. *The animals made a desperate attempt to escape the forest fire.* —**des•per•ate•ly** adv. —**des•per•ate•ness** n.

de•tect /dĭ tĕkt′/ v. **de•tect•ed, de•tect•ing, de•tects.** to notice or discover evidence of behavior or actions. *I could detect the sadness in his voice.* —**de•tect•a•ble** or **de•tect•i•ble** adj. —**de•tect•er** n.

de•ter•mine /dĭ tûr′ mĭn/ v. **de•ter•mined, de•ter•min•ing, de•ter•mines.** to decide firmly. *She determined to make the trip with me.*

de•ter•mined /dĭ tûr′ mĭnd/ adj. firm; stubborn. *The determined child refused help.* —**de•ter•mined•ly** adv. —**de•ter•mined•ness** n.

di•ag•nose /dī′ əg nōs′ or dī′ əg nōz′/ v. **di•ag•nosed, di•ag•nos•ing, di•ag•nos•es.** to examine and identify. *The doctor diagnosed the problem.*

di•men•sion /dĭ mĕn′ shən or dī mĕn′ shən/ n. a measure of height, length, or width. *What are the dimensions of your room?* —**di•men•sion•al** adj. —**di•men•sion•al•ly** adv.

di•rect¹ /dĭ rĕkt′ or dī rĕkt′/ adj. moving in a straight line. *Tell me the most direct route to your house.* —**di•rect•ly** adv. —**di•rect•ness** n.

di•rect² /dĭ rĕkt′ or dī rĕkt′/ v. **di•rect•ed, di•rect•ing, di•rects.** to move toward a goal. *The teacher directs the work of the class.*

di•rect³ /dĭ rĕkt′ or dī rĕkt′/ v. **di•rect•ed, di•rect•ing, di•rects.** to aim; to cause to move in a certain way or direction. *The painter directed light onto his work.*

dis•as•ter /dĭ zăs′ tər/ n. a destructive event. *The fire at the hotel was a disaster.*

dis•col•or /dĭs kŭl′ ər/ v. **dis•col•ored, dis•col•or•ing, dis•col•ors.** to change or spoil the color; to stain. *The spilled juice discolored the tablecloth.*

dis•col•or•a•tion /dĭs kŭl′ ə rā′ shən/ n. a stain. *There was some discoloration in the cloth.*

dis•grace•ful /dĭs grās′ fəl/ adj. shameful. *Making fun of someone is disgraceful.* —**dis•grace•ful•ly** adv. —**dis•grace•ful•ness** n.

dis•lo•cate /dĭs′ lō kāt′ or dĭs lō′ kāt/ v. **dis•lo•cat•ed, dis•lo•cat•ing, dis•lo•cates.** to put out of place. *The flooding river dislocated the people who lived nearby.* —**dis•lo•ca•tion** n.

dis•please /dĭs plēz′/ v. **dis•pleased, dis•pleas•ing, dis•pleas•es.** to cause annoyance; to make unhappy. *Gossip displeases me.* —**dis•pleas•ing•ly** adv.

dis•re•spect•ful /dĭs′ rĭ spĕkt′ fəl/ adj. rude and inconsiderate. *Talking loudly during a concert is disrespectful.* —**dis•re•spect•ful•ly** adv. —**dis•re•spect•ful•ness** n.

dis•tance¹ /dĭs′ təns/ n. a stretch of space. *He can run the full distance.*

dis•tance² /dĭs′ təns/ v. **dis•tanced, dis•tanc•ing, dis•tanc•es.** to keep away. *Try to distance yourself from trouble.*

dis•tinct¹ /dĭ stĭngkt′/ adj. different. *The baby had a distinct cry when he was hungry.* —**dis•tinct•ly** adv.

dis•tinct² /dĭ stĭngkt′/ adj. easily noticed by senses or intellect. *A distinct odor was coming from the store.* —**dis•tinct•ly** adv.

dis•tin•guish¹ /dĭ stĭng′ gwĭsh/ v. **dis•tin•guished, dis•tin•guish•ing, dis•tin•guish•es.** to recognize the difference. *Only their mother could distinguish one twin from the other.* —**dis•tin•guish•a•ble** adj. —**dis•tin•guish•a•bly** adv.

dis•tin•guish² /dĭ stĭng′ gwĭsh/ *v.*
**dis•tin•guished, dis•tin•guish•ing,
dis•tin•guish•es.** to make noticeable. *She
distinguished herself in math class.*
—**dis•tin•guish•a•ble** *adj.*
—**dis•tin•guish•a•bly** *adv.*

do•mes•tic¹ /də měs′ tĭk/ *adj.* relating to family
or household. *We all help with the domestic
chores.* —**do•mes•ti•cal•ly** *adv.*

do•mes•tic² /də měs′ tĭk/ *adj.* tame. *A lion is not
a domestic animal.* —**do•mes•ti•cal•ly** *adv.*

dor•mi•to•ry /dôr′ mĭ tôr′ ē *or* dôr′ mĭ tōr′ ē/ *n.,
pl.* **dor•mi•to•ries.** a building for housing a
number of people. *I will stay in the dormitory
when I go to camp.*

drab /drăb/ *adj.* **drab•ber, drab•best.** dull. *The
office was decorated in drab colors.*
—**drab•ly** *adv.* —**drab•ness** *n.*

E

el•e•vate /ěl′ ə vāt′/ *v.* **el•e•vat•ed, el•e•vat•ing,
el•e•vates.** to raise; to lift. *The mechanic
elevated the car to change the tires.*

el•e•va•tion /ěl′ ə vā′ shən/ *n.* the act of raising
or lifting. *A large crane provided elevation
for the heavy monument.*

em•blem /ěm′ bləm/ *n.* a badge, symbol, or
design used for identification. *The emblem on
her shirt showed she was on the swim team.*

en•close /ěn klōz′/ *or* **in•close** /ĭn klōz′/ *v.*
en•closed, en•clos•ing, en•clos•es. to
surround; to envelop. *A fence encloses the
playground.*

en•light•en /ěn līt′ n/ *v.* **en•light•ened,
en•light•en•ing, en•light•ens.** to inform; to
make clearer. *Please enlighten me about the
dangers of poison ivy.*

ep•i•dem•ic /ěp′ ĭ děm′ ĭk/ *n.* a disease that
spreads rapidly. *There was a flu epidemic in
our school.*

e•rect¹ /ĭ rěkt′/ *v.* **e•rect•ed, e•rect•ing, e•rects.**
to build; to construct. *The townspeople will
erect a fountain in the park.*
—**e•rect•a•ble** *adj.* —**e•rect•ly** *adv.*
—**e•rect•ness** *n.*

e•rect² /ĭ rěkt′/ *adj.* in an upright position. *The
children practiced walking with erect posture.*
—**e•rect•a•ble** *adj.* —**e•rect•ly** *adv.*
—**e•rect•ness** *n.*

e•rup•tion /ĭ rŭp′ shən/ *n.* a sudden outburst or
explosion. *The eruption of the volcano filled
the sky with ashes.*

es•tate /ĭ stāt′/ *n.* a large piece of property,
usually with a large house. *They live on a
beautiful estate in the country.*

e•vade /ĭ vād′/ *v.* **e•vad•ed, e•vad•ing, e•vades.**
to avoid; to escape. *I evade injury by wearing
a bicycle helmet.*

ev•i•dence¹ /ěv′ ĭ dəns/ *n.* proof; facts or
information that serves as proof. *The
evidence against the criminal was enough for
a long jail sentence.*

ev•i•dence² /ěv′ ĭ dəns/ *v.* **ev•i•denced,
ev•i•denc•ing, ev•i•denc•es.** to show clearly.
*Their good grades evidenced their hours of
studying.* **in ev•i•dence** *idiom.* plain to see;
conspicuous. *The effects of the storm were
very much in evidence.*

ex•am•ine /ĭg zăm′ ĭn/ *v.* **ex•am•ined,
ex•am•in•ing, ex•am•ines.** to look at closely;
to check the condition. *The nurse examined
the patient's eyes.* —**ex•am•in•er** *n.*

ex•ca•vate /ěk′ skə vāt′/ *v.* **ex•ca•vat•ed,
ex•ca•vat•ing, ex•ca•vates.** to dig out; to
uncover. *We excavated the time capsule.*

ex•clude /ĭk sklo͞od′/ *v.* **ex•clud•ed, ex•clud•ing,
ex•cludes.** to keep out; to prevent from being
a part of. *The club cannot exclude them from
becoming members.*

ex•hib•it¹ /ĭg zĭb′ ĭt *or* ěg zĭb′ ĭt/ *v.* **ex•hib•it•ed,
ex•hib•it•ing, ex•hib•its.** to show for all to
see. *The museum will exhibit quilts made by
local artists.* —**ex•hib•it•or** *or* **ex•hib•it•er** *n.*

ex•hib•it² /ĭg zĭb′ ĭt *or* ěg zĭb′ ĭt/ *v.* **ex•hib•it•ed,
ex•hib•it•ing, ex•hib•its.** to introduce in
court as part of a trial. *The attorney exhibited
two pictures during the trial.* —**ex•hib•it•or**
or **ex•hib•it•er** *n.*

ex•hib•it³ /ĭg zĭb′ ĭt *or* ěg zĭb′ ĭt/ *n.* a public
show. *The museum has an exhibit of old cars.*

ex•pand /ĭk spănd′/ v. **ex•pand•ed, ex•pand•ing, ex•pands.** to increase in size or amount. *Our teacher wants us to expand our vocabulary.* —**ex•pand•a•ble** adj.

ex•pect[1] /ĭk spĕkt′/ v. **ex•pect•ed, ex•pect•ing, ex•pects.** to look for as likely to happen. *I expect my cousins to arrive soon.* —**ex•pect•a•ble** adj. —**ex•pect•ed•ly** adv. —**ex•pect•ed•ness** n.

ex•pect[2] /ĭk spĕkt′/ v. **ex•pect•ed, ex•pect•ing, ex•pects.** to assume or suppose. *I expect you will want a new shirt for the party.* —**ex•pect•a•ble** adj. —**ex•pect•ed•ly** adv. —**ex•pect•ed•ness** n.

ex•pect[3] /ĭk spĕkt′/ v. **ex•pect•ed, ex•pect•ing, ex•pects.** to require. *We expect an apology after your angry outburst.* —**ex•pect•a•ble** adj. —**ex•pect•ed•ly** adv. —**ex•pect•ed•ness** n.

ex•pe•di•tion /ĕk′ spĭ dĭsh′ ən/ n. a long journey. *The scientists went on an expedition to Greenland.*

ex•port /ĭk spôrt′ or ĕk′ spôrt/ v. **ex•port•ed, ex•port•ing, ex•ports.** to send to another country. *The United States exports a lot of wheat and corn.* —**ex•port•a•ble** adj. —**ex•port•a•bil•i•ty** n. —**ex•port•er** n.

F

fab•ric /făb′ rĭk/ n. cloth. *We bought soft fabric for a new jacket.*

fa•cial[1] /fā′ shəl/ adj. having to do with the face. *His facial expressions were funny.* —**fa•cial•ly** adv.

fa•cial[2] /fā′ shəl/ n. a treatment for the face. *After the facial, her skin felt very smooth.*

fa•cil•i•ty /fə sĭl′ ĭ tē/ n., pl. **fa•cil•i•ties.** something built for a particular function. *Our community has a great recreational facility.*

fa•mil•iar /fə mĭl′ yər/ adj. having knowledge about something. *I am familiar with that store.* —**fa•mil•iar•ly** adv.

fa•vor•a•ble /fā′ vər ə bəl or făv′ rə bəl/ adj. helpful; agreeable. *The weather looks favorable for sailing.* —**fa•vor•a•ble•ness** n. —**fa•vor•a•bly** adv.

fe•ro•cious /fə rō′ shəs/ adj. wild and fierce. *The kitten tried to act ferocious.* —**fe•ro•cious•ly** adv. —**fe•ro•cious•ness** n.

fe•ver•ish /fē′ vər ĭsh/ adj. having a high body temperature. *The baby was feverish.* —**fe•ver•ish•ly** adv. —**fe•ver•ish•ness** n.

for•eign /fôr′ ĭn or fŏr′ ĭn/ adj. from another country. *We have several foreign students in our class.* —**for•eign•ness** n.

fore•sight /fôr′ sīt′ or fŏr′ sīt/ n. the ability to see ahead. *It takes foresight to plan a successful vacation.*

form[1] /fôrm/ n. the shape and structure of something. *Try to describe the form of a pyramid.*

form[2] /fôrm/ v. **formed, form•ing, forms.** to give shape to something. *He formed the clay into a vase.* —**form•a•ble** adj. —**form•a•bil•i•ty** n.

for•mat[1] /fôr′ măt′/ n. a plan or design; an arrangement. *I'd like to change the format of my bedroom.*

for•mat[2] /fôr′ măt′/ v. **for•mat•ted, for•mat•ting, for•mats.** to plan or arrange something. *How would you like to format the school newspaper?*

for•ma•tion /fôr mā′ shən/ n. an arrangement; the way something is formed or grouped. *The band marched in a straight formation.* —**for•ma•tion•al** adj.

form•less /fôrm′ lĭs/ adj. shapeless. *The once formless water is now a beautiful ice sculpture.* —**form•less•ly** adv. —**form•less•ness** n.

for•tu•i•tous /fôr to͞o′ ĭ təs/ adj. lucky. *It was fortuitous that you found your lost keys.* —**for•tu•i•tous•ly** adv. —**for•tu•i•tous•ness** n.

for•tune[1] /fôr′ chən/ n. luck. *Did you have the good fortune of finding your lost kitten?*

for•tune[2] /fôr′ chən/ n. a large sum of money. *The new stadium cost a fortune.*

fos•sil /fŏs′ əl/ n. the hardened remains of plants or animals from long ago. *I found the fossil of a leaf in a large rock.*

frag•ile¹ /frăj′ əl *or* frăj′ īl/ *adj.* frail; easily broken. *Pack these fragile teacups very carefully.* —**frag•ile•ly** *adv.* —**fra•gil•i•ty** *n.* —**frag•ile•ness** *n.*

frag•ile² /frăj′ əl *or* frăj′ īl/ *adj.* frail; weak. *He was a bit fragile during his lengthy illness.* —**frag•ile•ly** *adv.* —**fra•gil•i•ty** *n.* —**frag•ile•ness** *n.*

frail•ty /frāl′ tē/ *n., pl.* **frail•ties.** a weakness; a fault. *The athlete didn't have a single physical frailty.*

fringe¹ /frĭnj/ *n.* a decorative border of hanging threads, cords, or strips. *The bottom of her skirt had a fringe.*

fringe² /frĭnj/ *n.* an outer edge or border. *A fringe of trees lined the park's boundary.*

fringe³ /frĭnj/ *v.* **fringed, fring•ing, fring•es.** to serve as a fringe or border. *Rosebushes fringed the garden.*

fron•tier /frŭn tîr′ *or* frŭn′ tîr/ *n.* an undeveloped area. *Early Americans explored new frontiers.*

fu•ri•ous /fyŏŏr′ ē əs/ *adj.* extremely angry. *I was furious when my new coat got muddy.* —**fu•ri•ous•ly** *adv.* —**fu•ri•ous•ness** *n.*

gen•er•ous /jĕn′ ər əs/ *adj.* not selfish; willing to share. *The child was generous with his toys.* —**gen•er•ous•ly** *adv.*

gen•ius /jēn′ yəs/ *n., pl.* **gen•ius•es.** a person with very high intelligence; extremely high mental or creative ability. *It will take a genius to solve this problem.*

gen•teel /jĕn tēl′/ *adj.* polite and well-mannered. *The elderly man and woman were so genteel.* —**gen•teel•ly** *adv.* —**gen•teel•ness** *n.*

gen•u•ine /jĕn′ yŏŏ ĭn/ *adj.* real; true; sincere. *Her friendship is genuine.* —**gen•u•ine•ly** *adv.* —**gen•u•ine•ness** *n.*

ge•og•ra•phy /jē ŏg′ rə fē/ *n., pl.* **ge•og•ra•phies.** the study of the earth and its physical features, such as continents, water, climate, and resources. *We will study the geography of South America.* —**ge•og•ra•pher** *n.*

ge•ol•o•gist /jē ŏl′ ə jĭst/ *n.* a scientist who studies the structure of the earth. *The geologist studied rock formations along the coastline.*

ge•o•met•ric /jē′ ə mĕt′ rĭk/ *or* **ge•o•met•ri•cal** /jē′ ə mĕt′ rĭ kəl/ *adj.* using simple shapes in design. *The artist cut the cloth into several geometric shapes.* —**ge•o•met•ri•cal•ly** *adv.*

germ /jûrm/ *n.* a tiny organism, especially one that can make people sick. *Some germs spread rapidly.*

ger•mi•nate /jûr′ mə nāt′/ *v.* **ger•mi•nat•ed, ger•mi•nat•ing, ger•mi•nates.** to make a seed grow. *The seeds will germinate with water and light.*

grace•ful /grās′ fəl/ *adj.* showing grace in movement or form. *The swan looked very graceful as it glided through the water.* —**grace•ful•ly** *adv.* —**grace•ful•ness** *n.*

gra•cious /grā′ shəs/ *adj.* showing kindness, courtesy, or tact. *A gracious woman gave her seat to a mother carrying a child.* —**gra•cious•ly** *adv.* —**gra•cious•ness** *n.*

grate•ful /grāt′ fəl/ *adj.* appreciative of things or actions received; expressing thanks. *The man was grateful for his warm coat during the snowstorm.* —**grate•ful•ly** *adv.* —**grate•ful•ness** *n.*

gru•el•ing *or* **gru•el•ling** /grŏŏ′ ə lĭng *or* grŏŏ′ lĭng/ *adj.* hard; exhausting. *The long walk home was grueling.* —**gru•el•ing•ly** *adv.*

haz•ard¹ /hăz′ ərd/ *n.* something that could cause harm or danger. *The hole in the middle of the street is a hazard.*

haz•ard² /hăz′ ərd/ *v.* **haz•ard•ed, haz•ard•ing, haz•ards.** to expose to danger. *Police officers and firefighters hazard their lives each day.*

head•way /hĕd′ wā/ *n.* forward movement. *We finally made some headway through the traffic.*

herb /ûrb *or* hûrb/ *n.* a plant that can be used for medicine or seasoning. *Some herbs are used to make soothing teas.*

hes•i•tant /hĕz′ ĭ tənt/ *adj.* not sure; doubtful; reluctant. *I was hesitant to cross the busy street.* —**hes•i•tant•ly** *adv.*

hor•rif•ic /hô rĭf′ ĭk *or* hŏ rĭf′ ĭk/ *adj.* shocking; terrifying. *She saw a horrific fire.* —**hor•rif•i•cal•ly** *adv.*

hum•ble¹ /hŭm′ bəl/ *adj.* **hum•bler, hum•blest.** modest; not proud. *It is often better to be humble than to brag too much.* —**hum•bly** *adv.* —**hum•ble•ness** *n.*

hum•ble² /hŭm′ bəl/ *v.* **hum•bled, hum•bling, hum•bles.** to cause to be modest. *Losing the game humbled the team.*

I

il•lu•mi•nate /ĭ lōō′ mə nāt′/ *v.* **il•lu•mi•nat•ed, il•lu•mi•nat•ing, il•lu•mi•nates.** to provide light; to make clear. *Sunshine illuminates the room.*

il•lus•trate /ĭl′ ə strāt′ *or* ĭ lŭs′ trāt′/ *v.* **il•lus•trat•ed, il•lus•trat•ing, il•lus•trates.** to make clear with pictures or examples. *The author also illustrated the story.*

im•mune /ĭ myōōn′/ *adj.* protected from a disease. *The dog was immune to the disease.*

im•mu•nize /ĭm′ yə nīz′/ *v.* **im•mu•nized, im•mu•niz•ing, im•mu•niz•es.** to protect from a disease. *It is important to immunize babies against illnesses.*

im•pass•a•ble /ĭm păs′ ə bəl/ *adj.* unable to be crossed. *Ice on the bridge made it impassable.* —**im•pass•a•bly** *adv.* —**im•pass•a•ble•ness** *n.* —**im•pass•a•bil•i•ty** *n.*

im•port /ĭm pôrt′ *or* ĭm′ pôrt/ *v.* **im•port•ed, im•port•ing, im•ports.** to bring goods in from another country. *The United States imports many goods from China.* —**im•port•a•ble** *adj.* —**im•port•a•bil•i•ty** *n.* —**im•port•er** *n.*

in•clude /ĭn klōōd′/ *v.* **in•clud•ed, in•clud•ing, in•cludes.** to allow to be part of. *I included all of my friends in the game.* —**in•clud•a•ble** *or* **in•clud•i•ble** *adj.*

in•con•sid•er•ate /ĭn′ kən sĭd′ ər ĭt/ *adj.* thoughtless; not thinking of others. *It is inconsiderate to slam doors.* —**in•con•sid•er•ate•ly** *adv.* —**in•con•sid•er•ate•ness** *n.* —**in•con•sid•er•a•tion** *n.*

in•di•vid•u•al¹ /ĭn′ də vĭj′ ōō əl/ *adj.* separate. *We have individual plans for dinner.* —**in•di•vid•u•al•ly** *adv.*

in•di•vid•u•al² /ĭn′ də vĭj′ ōō əl/ *n.* a single person or thing. *Each individual in our class will receive a book.*

in•fec•tion /ĭn fĕk′ shən/ *n.* an illness caused by germs. *The throat infection caused her to miss school for a week.*

in•se•cure /ĭn′ sĭ kyŏŏr′/ *adj.* not sure; uncertain. *He felt insecure on the skateboard.* —**in•se•cure•ly** *adv.* —**in•se•cu•ri•ty** *n.* —**in•se•cure•ness** *n.*

in•spect /ĭn spĕkt′/ *v.* **in•spect•ed, in•spect•ing, in•spects.** to review or examine. *The detective wanted to inspect all of the rooms in the hotel.* —**in•spec•tive** *adj.*

in•te•ri•or /ĭn tîr′ ē ər/ *n.* the inner part. *The interior of the house needs to be painted.*

in•vade¹ /ĭn vād′/ *v.* **in•vad•ed, in•vad•ing, in•vades.** to enter by force; to attack. *The soldiers invaded a village.* —**in•vad•er** *n.*

in•vade² /ĭn vād′/ *v.* **in•vad•ed, in•vad•ing, in•vades.** to overrun; to spread harm. *Flies invaded the house.* —**in•vad•er** *n.*

in•volve /ĭn vŏlv′/ *v.* **in•volved, in•volv•ing, in•volves.** to include or draw in. *What school activities are you involved in?* —**in•volve•ment** *n.*

ir•reg•u•lar¹ /ĭ rĕg′ yə lər/ *adj.* not evenly shaped or arranged; uneven. *The puzzle pieces had irregular shapes.* —**ir•reg•u•lar•ly** *adv.* —**ir•reg•u•lar•i•ty** *n.*

ir•reg•u•lar² /ĭ rĕg′ yə lər/ *adj.* different from the accepted rule or practice. *Our irregular class schedule was a result of this morning's assembly.* —**ir•reg•u•lar•ly** *adv.* —**ir•reg•u•lar•i•ty** *n.*

PRONUNCIATION KEY	
/ă/	pat
/ā/	pay
/â/	care
/ä/	father
/är/	far
/ĕ/	pet
/ē/	be
/ĭ/	pit
/ī/	pie
/îr/	pier
/ŏ/	mop
/ō/	toe
/ô/	paw, for
/oi/	noise
/ou/	out
/ŏŏ/	look
/ōō/	boot
/ŭ/	cut
/ûr/	urge
/th/	thin
/th/	this
/hw/	what
/zh/	vision
/ə/	about
	item
	pencil
	gallop
	circus
/ər/	butter

i•so•late /ī' sə lāt′/ v. **i•so•lat•ed, i•so•lat•ing, i•so•lates.** to separate from others. *We had to isolate the sick puppy.* —**i•so•la•tor** n.

junc•tion /jŭngk′ shən/ n. a place where two roads or rail lines join or cross. *An accident occurred at the railroad junction.* —**junc•tion•al** adj.

leg•i•ble /lĕj′ ə bəl/ adj. can be read easily. *Be sure to use legible handwriting.* —**leg•i•bly** adv. —**leg•i•bil•i•ty** n. —**leg•i•ble•ness** n.

lime•stone /līm′ stōn′/ n. a type of rock. *We built a patio out of limestone.*

lo•cal[1] /lō′ kəl/ adj. of the community. *We shop at the local grocery store.* —**lo•cal•ly** adv.

lo•cal[2] /lō′ kəl/ n. one who lives in a certain area. *Ask the locals about the best places to eat.*

lo•cale /lō kăl′/ n. a particular place. *The locale of the movie is New York City.*

lo•cal•ism /lō′ kə līz′ əm/ n. the custom of a certain area. *Their localism of an open market is quite different from my neighborhood grocery store.*

lo•cal•i•ty /lō kăl′ ĭ tē/ n. a neighborhood. *The stadium is in the locality of the school.*

lo•cal•ize /lō′ kə līz′/ v. **lo•cal•ized, lo•cal•iz•ing, lo•cal•iz•es.** to restrict to a particular place or area. *The infection was localized in my hand.*

lo•co•mo•tion /lō′ kə mō′ shən/ n. the act of moving from one place to another. *Locomotion by dogsled is a good way to travel on snow.*

loy•al /loi′ əl/ adj. faithful. *The dog was loyal to its owner.* —**loy•al•ly** adv.

lu•mi•nous /lōō′ mə nəs/ adj. giving off light; shining. *The stars were luminous against the night sky.* —**lu•mi•nous•ly** adv. —**lu•mi•nous•ness** n.

lu•nar /lōō′ nər/ adj. relating to the moon. *We watched a lunar eclipse last night.*

man•a•cle[1] /măn′ ə kəl/ n. handcuff; restraint. *The thief was taken away wearing a pair of manacles.*

man•a•cle[2] /măn′ ə kəl/ v. **man•a•cled, man•a•cling, man•a•cles.** to put on restraints. *A police officer manacled the prisoner.*

man•i•cure[1] /măn′ ĭ kyŏŏr′/ n. a cosmetic treatment for hands and fingernails. *She got a manicure before attending the party.*

man•i•cure[2] /măn′ ĭ kyŏŏr′/ v. **man•i•cured, man•i•cur•ing, man•i•cures.** to trim, clean, and polish the fingernails. *I manicure my fingernails every other week.*

man•u•al /măn′ yŏŏ əl/ adj. worked with the hands. *The machine has manual controls for adjusting speed.* —**man•u•al•ly** adv.

man•u•fac•ture /măn′ yə făk′ chər/ v. **man•u•fac•tured, man•u•fac•tur•ing, man•u•fac•tures.** to make with a machine. *The small company manufactures balloons.*

mar•vel•ous or **mar•vel•lous** /mär′ və ləs/ adj. causing wonder; amazing. *The personal computer is a marvelous invention.* —**mar•vel•ous•ly** adv. —**mar•vel•ous•ness** n.

ma•ter•nal[1] /mə tûr′ nəl/ adj. motherly. *Her maternal actions were very comforting.* —**ma•ter•nal•ly** adv.

ma•ter•nal[2] /mə tûr′ nəl/ adj. related through a mother. *I look like my maternal grandmother.* —**ma•ter•nal•ly** adv.

ma•ter•ni•ty /mə tûr′ nĭ tē/ adj. having to do with motherhood. *I visited my friend in the maternity ward of the hospital.*

ma•tri•arch /mā′ trē ärk′/ n. the female head of a family. *My grandmother is the matriarch of our large family.* —**ma•tri•ar•chal** adj.

me•te•or•ite /mē′ tē ə rīt′/ n. a chunk of solid matter that falls from space. *A meteorite landed near the farmhouse.*

me•te•or•ol•o•gy /mē′ tē ə rŏl′ ə jē/ n. the study of weather. *If you study meteorology, you can learn to track storms.* —**me•te•or•ol•o•gist** n.

mi•grate /mī′ grāt/ *v.* **mi•grat•ed, mi•grat•ing, mi•grates.** to move from one place to another. *Some birds migrate between North America and South America.*

mi•gra•tion /mī grā′ shən/ *n.* the act of moving from one place to another. *The migration of workers in search of jobs was common during the 1930s.*

mis•er•y /mĭz′ ə rē/ *n., pl.* **mis•er•ies.** suffering; distress. *He was in misery with his bad cold.*

mis•for•tune /mĭs fôr′ chən/ *n.* bad luck. *It was her misfortune to spill chocolate on her new dress.*

mo•bile¹ /mō′ bəl *or* mō′ bēl′ *or* mō′ bīl′/ *adj.* able to move. *He was less mobile after his surgery.* —**mo•bil•i•ty** *n.*

mo•bile² /mō′ bēl′/ *n.* a kind of sculpture with moving parts. *A mobile hung above the baby's crib.*

mod•est /mŏd′ ĭst/ *adj.* reserved; not showy. *The winners were modest about their success.* —**mod•est•ly** *adv.*

murk•y /mûr′ kē/ *adj.* **murk•i•er, murk•i•est.** gloomy; dark. *The river water was murky.* —**murk•i•ly** *adv.* —**murk•i•ness** *n.*

N

no•ble /nō′ bəl/ *adj.* **no•bler, no•blest.** admirable; courageous. *He worked for a noble cause.* —**no•ble•ness** *n.* —**no•bly** *adv.*

no•tice•a•ble /nō′ tĭ sə bəl/ *adj.* easily seen. *The wrinkles in his shirt were really noticeable.* —**no•tice•a•bly** *adv.*

O

ob•serve¹ /əb zûrv′/ *v.* **ob•served, ob•serv•ing, ob•serves.** to notice or watch. *We observe the animals at the wildlife center.* —**ob•serv•ing•ly** *adv.*

ob•serve² /əb zûrv′/ *v.* **ob•served, ob•serv•ing, ob•serves.** to obey or comply with. *We will observe all the rules of the game.* —**ob•serv•ing•ly** *adv.*

ob•serve³ /əb zûrv′/ *v.* **ob•served, ob•serv•ing, ob•serves.** to celebrate or give honor to a day or event. *We will observe my sister's birthday with a party.* —**ob•serv•ing•ly** *adv.*

ob•sta•cle /ŏb′ stə kəl/ *n.* something in the way. *I can't open the door because there is an obstacle in the way.*

ob•vi•ous /ŏb′ vē əs/ *adj.* easy to see or understand. *His red shirt was quite obvious next to the white uniforms.* —**ob•vi•ous•ly** *adv.* —**ob•vi•ous•ness** *n.*

P

pace /pās/ *n.* the rate of speed of walking or running. *It was hard to keep up with his fast pace.*

par•al•lel¹ /păr′ ə lĕl′/ *adj.* lying in the same plane and being equally distant. *Draw parallel lines on your paper.*

par•al•lel² /păr′ ə lĕl′/ *v.* **par•al•leled, par•al•lel•ing, par•al•els** *or* **par•al•lelled, par•al•lel•ling, par•al•lels.** to be in the same plane and equally distant. *The two streets parallel each other.*

par•tic•i•pate /pär tĭs′ ə pāt′/ *v.* **par•tic•i•pat•ed, par•tic•i•pat•ing, par•tic•i•pates.** to join with others to do something. *Our class participates in the school art contest.* —**par•tic•i•pa•tive** *adj.* —**par•tic•i•pa•tor** *n.*

par•tic•i•pa•tion /pär tĭs′ ə pā′ shən/ *n.* the act of taking part in something. *His participation in sports keeps him quite busy.*

pas•sage /păs′ ĭj/ *n.* a path or route. *The trail took us through a rocky passage.*

pas•sive /păs′ ĭv/ *adj.* accepting without resistance. *He was a passive member of the committee.* —**pas•sive•ly** *adv.* —**pas•sive•ness** *n.*

pa•ter•nal¹ /pə tûr′ nəl/ *adj.* fatherly. *My older brother sometimes gives out paternal advice.* —**pa•ter•nal•ly** *adv.*

pa•ter•nal² /pə tûr′ nəl/ *adj.* related through a father. *My paternal grandfather was from Germany.* —**pa•ter•nal•ly** *adv.*

PRONUNCIATION KEY	
/ă/	p**a**t
/ā/	p**ay**
/â/	c**a**re
/ä/	f**a**ther
/är/	f**ar**
/ĕ/	p**e**t
/ē/	b**e**
/ĭ/	p**i**t
/ī/	p**ie**
/îr/	p**ier**
/ŏ/	m**o**p
/ō/	t**oe**
/ô/	p**aw**, f**or**
/oi/	n**oi**se
/ou/	**ou**t
/o͝o/	l**oo**k
/o͞o/	b**oo**t
/ŭ/	c**u**t
/ûr/	**ur**ge
/th/	**th**in
/th/	**th**is
/hw/	**wh**at
/zh/	vi**s**ion
/ə/	**a**bout
	item
	penc**i**l
	gall**o**p
	circ**u**s
/ər/	butt**er**

pa•tient¹ /pā′ shənt/ *adj.* willing to wait; willing to put up with problems. *The shopper was patient as he waited in line.* —**pa•tient•ly** adv.

pa•tient² /pā′ shənt/ *n.* someone who gets medical attention. *The patient was waiting to see the doctor.*

pa•tri•arch /pā′ trē ärk′/ *n.* the male head of a family. *The patriarch of the tribe was brave and strong.* —**pa•tri•ar•chal** adj.

pa•tron /pā′ trən/ *n.* a regular customer. *My aunt is a patron of art galleries.*

ped•al¹ /pĕd′ l/ *n.* a lever worked with the foot. *The bike pedal needed some repair.*

ped•al² /pĕd′ l/ *v.* **ped•aled, ped•al•ing, ped•als** *or* **ped•alled, ped•al•ling, ped•als.** to operate with the feet. *It is hard to pedal my bike up hills.*

ped•es•tal /pĕd′ ĭ stəl/ *n.* a base for holding something. *The statue stood on a large pedestal made of stone.*

pe•des•tri•an /pə dĕs′ trē ən/ *n.* a person traveling on foot. *The pedestrian used the crosswalk.*

ped•i•cure /pĕd′ ĭ kyoor′/ *n.* a cosmetic treatment for feet and toenails. *She put on her sandals after the pedicure.*

pen•in•su•la /pə nĭn′ syə lə *or* pə nĭn′ sə lə/ *n.* a piece of land that juts out into water but remains connected to land. *The state of Florida is a peninsula.*

per•ma•nent /pûr′ mə nənt/ *adj.* lasting a very long time. *Campers label their clothes with permanent ink.* —**per•ma•nent•ly** adv.

per•son•al /pûr′ sə nəl/ *adj.* relating to a particular person. *I write personal things in my diary.*

per•spec•tive¹ /pər spĕk′ tĭv/ *n.* a point of view. *From my perspective, the book was good.*

per•spec•tive² /pər spĕk′ tĭv/ *n.* a way to show dimension. *The artist's use of color gave perspective to the painting.*

phy•si•cian /fĭ zĭsh′ ən/ *n.* a medical doctor. *My physician met me at the hospital.*

pleas•ant¹ /plĕz′ ənt/ *adj.* **pleas•ant•er, pleas•ant•est.** pleasing; nice. *The quietness of the room was pleasant.* —**pleas•ant•ly** adv. —**pleas•ant•ness** n.

pleas•ant² /plĕz′ ənt/ *adj.* **pleas•ant•er, pleas•ant•est.** fair and comfortable. *We enjoyed the pleasant weather.* —**pleas•ant•ly** adv. —**pleas•ant•ness** n.

pleas•ure /plĕzh′ ər/ *n.* a source of enjoyment. *Having lunch with friends is such a pleasure.*

po•di•a•trist /pə dī′ ə trĭst/ *n.* a doctor who treats feet. *The podiatrist told him to wear a special kind of shoe.*

pol•lute /pə loot′/ *v.* **pol•lut•ed, pol•lut•ing, pol•lutes.** to make impure or harmful to living things. *We should not pollute our rivers.* —**pol•lut•er** n.

pop•u•lar /pŏp′ yə lər/ *adj.* liked by many people. *That movie star is popular among teens.* —**pop•u•lar•ly** adv.

pop•u•la•tion /pŏp′ yə lā′ shən/ *n.* all the people in a particular place. *The population of the city has grown in the past few years.*

port•a•ble /pôr′ tə bəl/ *adj.* capable of being carried. *He took his portable radio everywhere.* —**port•a•bly** adv. —**port•a•ble•ness** n. —**port•a•bil•i•ty** n.

por•ter /pôr′ tər/ *n.* someone who carries luggage. *Give your luggage to the porter at the hotel.*

pre•cious /prĕsh′ əs/ *adj.* dear; beloved. *She is such a precious baby.* —**pre•cious•ly** adv. —**pre•cious•ness** n.

pre•scrip•tion /prĭ skrĭp′ shən/ *n.* a written instruction from a doctor to a patient for medicine or for a particular treatment. *The doctor wrote a prescription for cold medicine.*

pre•serve¹ /prĭ zûrv′/ *v.* **pre•served, pre•serv•ing, pre•serves.** to save; to protect. *Conservation groups work to preserve wilderness areas.* —**pre•serv•er** n.

pre•serve² /prĭ zûrv′/ *v.* **pre•served, pre•serv•ing, pre•serves.** to prepare for future use. *My mom will preserve peaches by canning them.* —**pre•serv•er** n.

pre•view¹ /prē′ vyoo′/ *n.* something seen in advance. *We saw a preview of the movie.*

pre•view² /prē′ vyoo′/ *v.* **pre•viewed, pre•view•ing, pre•views.** to show in advance. *The theater previewed two films that will soon be released.*

pri•va•cy /prī′ və sē/ *n.* the state of being alone. *She likes privacy when she is studying.*

pro•mote¹ /prə mōt′/ *v.* **pro•mot•ed, pro•mot•ing, pro•motes.** to raise to a higher level; to advance. *The teacher will promote her fourth-grade students to the fifth grade.*

pro•mote² /prə mōt′/ *v.* **pro•mot•ed, pro•mot•ing, pro•motes.** to help the growth or development of. *Daily brushing and flossing promote healthy teeth and gums.*

pro•mo•tion /prə mō′ shən/ *n.* the act of raising to a higher level. *The manager gave my brother a promotion.*

pro•vide¹ /prə vīd′/ *v.* **pro•vid•ed, pro•vid•ing, pro•vides.** to furnish or make available. *The boys provided food for the party.* —**pro•vid•er** *n.*

pro•vide² /prə vīd′/ *v.* **pro•vid•ed, pro•vid•ing, pro•vides.** to furnish a livelihood. *Parents want to provide well for their families.* —**pro•vid•er** *n.*

prov•ince /prŏv′ ĭns/ *n.* a subdivision of a country. *Canada is divided into provinces.*

pub•lic¹ /pŭb′ lĭk/ *adj.* for use by everyone; not private. *There are many public swimming pools in our community.* —**pub•lic•ness** *n.*

pub•lic² /pŭb′ lĭk/ *n.* the community. *The police would not give out information on the crime to the public.* —**pub•lic•ness** *n.*

pub•lic•i•ty /pŭ blĭs′ ĭ tē/ *n.* news given out to get attention. *There was much publicity for the new movie.*

R

ra•vine /rə vēn′/ *n.* a deep gully caused by running water. *The heavy rainfall formed a ravine between the two houses.*

re•as•sure /rē′ ə shŏŏr′/ *v.* **re•as•sured, re•as•sur•ing, re•as•sures.** to restore confidence. *We reassure the students that they are doing a good job.* —**re•as•sur•ing•ly** *adv.* —**re•as•sur•ance** *n.*

rec•tan•gu•lar /rĕk tăng′ gyə lər/ *adj.* having four sides with four right angles. *The fireplace opening was rectangular.*

re•gion /rē′ jən/ *n.* a large area. *They live in a very cold region of the world.*

reg•u•lar /rĕg′ yə lər/ *adj.* usual; normal. *The building had a regular shape.* —**reg•u•lar•ly** *adv.*

re•lo•cate /rē lō′ kāt/ *v.* **re•lo•cat•ed, re•lo•cat•ing, re•lo•cates.** to establish in a new place. *We relocated to Kansas to be closer to my grandparents.*

re•lo•ca•tion /rē′ lō kā′ shən/ *n.* the act of establishing in a new place. *The relocation of the library was a good decision.*

rem•e•dy¹ /rĕm′ ĭ dē/ *n., pl.* **rem•e•dies.** something that relieves pain. *The nurse had a remedy for headaches.*

rem•e•dy² /rĕm′ ĭ dē/ *v.* **rem•e•died, rem•e•dy•ing, rem•e•dies.** to relieve or cure. *My dad called to see if the doctor could remedy his backache.*

rep•u•ta•tion /rĕp′ yə tā′ shən/ *n.* the qualities for which someone or something is known. *Hal has a reputation for arriving late.*

re•sem•ble /rĭ zĕm′ bəl/ *v.* **re•sem•bled, re•sem•bling, re•sem•bles.** to be alike or nearly alike. *The baby kittens resemble yellow balls of fur.*

res•er•voir /rĕz′ ər vwär′ *or* rĕz′ ər vwôr′/ *n.* a natural or artificial place for storing water; a large supply. *The water in the town reservoir is almost gone.*

re•treat¹ /rĭ trēt′/ *v.* **re•treat•ed, re•treat•ing, re•treats.** to withdraw from danger or move back. *The children retreated to camp when the storm clouds appeared.*

re•treat² /rĭ trēt′/ *n.* a quiet place to withdraw to. *The cabin in the woods is our retreat.*

ri•val¹ /rī′ vəl/ *n.* a competitor. *My rival in the race ran faster than I did.*

ri•val² /rī′ vəl/ *v.* **ri•valed, ri•val•ing, ri•vals** *or* **ri•valled, ri•val•ling, ri•vals.** to compete with. *The two students rivaled for the title of best speller.*

PRONUNCIATION KEY	
/ă/	pat
/ā/	pay
/â/	care
/ä/	father
/är/	far
/ĕ/	pet
/ē/	be
/ĭ/	pit
/ī/	pie
/îr/	pier
/ŏ/	mop
/ō/	toe
/ô/	paw, for
/oi/	noise
/ou/	out
/ŏŏ/	look
/ōō/	boot
/ŭ/	cut
/ûr/	urge
/th/	thin
/th/	this
/hw/	what
/zh/	vision
/ə/	about
	item
	pencil
	gallop
	circus
/ər/	butter

ro•tate /rō′ tāt/ v. **ro•tat•ed, ro•tat•ing, ro•tates.** to spin on an axis. *The fan blades rotate rapidly.*

ro•ta•tion /rō tā′ shən/ n. the act of spinning on an axis. *One rotation of the earth takes twenty-four hours.*

ru•ral /roor′ əl/ adj. relating to a country area. *We live in a rural area one hundred miles south of Chicago.* —**ru•ral•ly** adv.

S

san•i•tar•y /săn′ ĭ tĕr′ ē/ adj. free from dirt, germs, or bacteria. *Surgeons scrub their hands to make sure they are sanitary.* —**san•i•tar•i•ly** adv.

san•i•tize /săn′ ĭ tīz′/ v. **san•i•tized, san•i•tiz•ing, san•i•tiz•es.** to clean germs from something. *Make sure to sanitize your hands before preparing dinner.*

scan¹ /skăn/ v. **scanned, scan•ning, scans.** to look over an area rapidly but thoroughly. *Dad began to scan the want ads.* —**scan•na•ble** adj. —**scan•ner** n.

scan² /skăn/ v. **scanned, scan•ning, scans.** to search electronically. *Scientists scan the ocean floor with sonar equipment.* —**scan•na•ble** adj. —**scan•ner** n.

se•cu•ri•ty /sĭ kyoor′ ĭ tē/ n., pl. **se•cu•ri•ties.** freedom from danger; safety. *The baby responded to the security of his father's strong arms.*

shim•mer /shĭm′ ər/ v. **shim•mered, shim•mer•ing, shim•mers.** to shine with a flickering light. *The fireflies shimmer in the dark.* —**shim•mer•y** adj.

shuf•fle¹ /shŭf′ əl/ v. **shuf•fled, shuf•fling, shuf•fles.** to drag or slide the feet along the ground when walking. *The old woman shuffled down the hallway.*

shuf•fle² /shŭf′ əl/ v. **shuf•fled, shuf•fling, shuf•fles.** to mix or stir. *We took turns shuffling the cards before each game.*

siege /sēj/ n. the surrounding of a town or fortress; a lengthy attack. *After a ten-day siege, the fort finally surrendered.*

sink•hole /sĭngk′ hōl′/ n. a sunken place in the earth. *The small stream disappeared into a sinkhole.*

so•cial¹ /sō′ shəl/ adj. enjoying the company of others. *The social behavior of the salesman helped him gain new customers.* —**so•cial•ly** adv.

so•cial² /sō′ shəl/ n. an informal gathering. *There is an ice cream social this weekend.*

so•ci•e•ty¹ /sə sī′ ĭ tē/ n., pl. **so•ci•e•ties.** a group of people with shared traditions and culture. *In U.S. society, people have certain freedoms that cannot be taken away.*

so•ci•e•ty² /sə sī′ ĭ tē/ n., pl. **so•ci•e•ties.** a group of people with the same interests. *Our school's literary society meets once each month.*

spe•cif•ic /spĭ sĭf′ ĭk/ adj. explicit or definite. *He asked for a specific amount of money.* —**spe•cif•i•cal•ly** adv.

spec•i•men /spĕs′ ə mən/ n. a sample. *The nurse took a blood specimen to the lab.*

stance¹ /stăns/ n. posture or position. *The old horse had a strange stance.*

stance² /stăns/ n. an attitude; a position. *What is your stance on the issue?*

sta•tion¹ /stā′ shən/ n. a place where a service is provided. *We need to stop at the gas station.*

sta•tion² /stā′ shən/ v. **sta•tioned, sta•tion•ing, sta•tions.** to assign to a place. *The king stationed a guard at the gate.*

sta•tion•ar•y /stā′ shə nĕr′ ē/ adj. not moving. *I ride a stationary bicycle when it's too cold to ride outside.*

sta•tion•er•y /stā′ shə nĕr′ ē/ n. writing paper. *He wrote a letter on his new stationery.*

stel•lar¹ /stĕl′ ər/ adj. relating to stars. *The night sky was a stellar display.*

stel•lar² /stĕl′ ər/ adj. outstanding. *The musician gave a stellar performance.*

stin•gy /stĭn′ jē/ adj. **stin•gi•er, stin•gi•est.** unwilling to give things or spend money. *They were stingy with their money.* —**stin•gi•ly** adv. —**stin•gi•ness** n.

strait¹ /strāt/ n. a channel of water that connects two larger bodies of water. *The ship sailed through the narrow strait into open water.*

strait² /strāt/ *n.* distress; difficulty; trouble. *We were in desperate straits without electricity.*

stur•dy /stûr′ dē/ *adj.* **stur•di•er, stur•di•est.** stout; firm; substantial. *The coat was made of a sturdy material.* —**stur•di•ly** *adv.* —**stur•di•ness** *n.*

sur•geon /sûr′ jən/ *n.* a doctor who performs operations. *The surgeon will take out my appendix.*

sur•pass /sər păs′/ *v.* **sur•passed, sur•pass•ing, sur•pass•es.** to go beyond. *The magic show surpassed our expectations.*

syn•thet•ic /sĭn thĕt′ ĭk/ *adj.* not made in or from nature or natural materials; made by people. *Some clothing is made of synthetic material.* —**syn•thet•i•cal•ly** *adv.*

— Ⓣ —

tel•e•vise /tĕl′ ə vīz′/ *v.* **tel•e•vised, tel•e•vis•ing, tel•e•vises.** to show on television. *We will watch the game if they televise it.*

tor•ment¹ /tôr′ mĕnt′/ *n.* great physical pain; mental anguish. *The headache caused her great torment.* —**tor•men•tor** *n.*

tor•ment² /tôr mĕnt′ or tôr′ mĕnt′/ *v.* **tor•ment•ed, tor•ment•ing, tor•ments.** to cause pain or mental anguish. *Terrible nightmares tormented her.* —**tor•men•tor** *n.*

tor•ment³ /tôr mĕnt′ or tôr′ mĕnt′/ *v.* **tor•ment•ed, tor•ment•ing, tor•ments.** to annoy. *The flies torment the cattle.* —**tor•men•tor** *n.*

tox•ic /tŏk′ sĭk/ *adj.* poisonous. *He was very sick from breathing the toxic smoke.*

trans•par•ent¹ /trăns pâr′ ənt/ *adj.* easy to see through. *The fabric for the bridal veil was transparent.* —**trans•par•ent•ly** *adv.*

trans•par•ent² /trăns pâr′ ənt/ *adj.* easy to understand or detect. *The lie the child told was transparent.* —**trans•par•ent•ly** *adv.*

trans•port /trăns pôrt′/ *v.* **trans•port•ed, trans•port•ing, trans•ports.** to carry from one place to another. *The truck transported mail overnight.* —**trans•port•a•ble** *adj.* —**trans•por•tive** *adj.* —**trans•port•a•bil•i•ty** *n.* —**trans•port•er** *n.*

trans•por•ta•tion /trăns′ pər tā′ shən/ *n.* the act of carrying from one place to another. *The school provides bus transportation for many students.*

trek¹ /trĕk/ *v.* **trekked, trek•king, treks.** to travel a slow and difficult journey. *The arctic explorers trekked up the steep and icy slopes.* —**trek•ker** *n.*

trek² /trĕk/ *n.* a slow, often difficult journey. *Our trek up the mountain made us very tired.* —**trek•ker** *n.*

trem•or¹ /trĕm′ ər/ *n.* a shaking movement. *I felt a tremor just before the earthquake.*

trem•or² /trĕm′ ər/ *n.* a muscle twitch. *Her hand had a slight tremor.*

tres•pass /trĕs′ pəs or trĕs′ păs′/ *v.* **tres•passed, tres•pass•ing, tres•pass•es.** to enter without permission. *Do not trespass on private property.* —**tres•pass•er** *n.*

— Ⓤ —

un•for•tu•nate /ŭn fôr′ chə nĭt/ *adj.* unlucky. *The unfortunate accident caused her to fear trains.* —**un•for•tu•nate•ly** *adv.*

u•ni•form¹ /yo͞o′ nə fôrm′/ *adj.* the same; unchanging. *The bricks were uniform in size.* —**u•ni•form•ly** *adv.* —**u•ni•for•mi•ty** *n.*

u•ni•form² /yo͞o′ nə fôrm′/ *n.* clothing that identifies a particular group. *The nurse wore a white uniform.*

ur•ban /ûr′ bən/ *adj.* relating to a city. *The urban streets were crowded with people.*

PRONUNCIATION KEY	
/ă/	pat
/ā/	pay
/â/	care
/ä/	father
/är/	far
/ĕ/	pet
/ē/	be
/ĭ/	pit
/ī/	pie
/îr/	pier
/ŏ/	mop
/ō/	toe
/ô/	paw, for
/oi/	noise
/ou/	out
/o͝o/	look
/o͞o/	boot
/ŭ/	cut
/ûr/	urge
/th/	thin
/th/	this
/hw/	what
/zh/	vision
/ə/	about
	item
	pencil
	gallop
	circus
/ər/	butter

vac•ci•nate /văk′ sə nāt′/ *v.* **vac•ci•nat•ed, vac•ci•nat•ing, vac•ci•nates.** to give an injection made from weak or dead germs that prevents a disease. *Our dog is vaccinated once a year.*

vac•cine /văk sēn′ *or* văk′ sēn′/ *n.* an injection made from weak or dead germs that prevents a disease. *There wasn't enough flu vaccine for all the doctor's patients.*

van•ish[1] /văn′ ĭsh/ *v.* **van•ished, van•ish•ing, van•ish•es.** to disappear. *The magician's doves seemed to vanish into thin air.*

van•ish[2] /văn′ ĭsh/ *v.* **van•ished, van•ish•ing, van•ish•es.** to disappear from existence. *The typewriter is vanishing with the popularity of computers.*

vi•sa /vē′ zə/ *n.* an official permission stamp allowing a traveler to enter or exit a certain country. *The officer checked my visa before allowing me into his country.*

vi•su•al[1] /vĭzh′ o͞o əl/ *adj.* having to do with sight. *His visual range is considered 20/20.* —**vi•su•al•ly** *adv.*

vi•su•al[2] /vĭzh′ o͞o əl/ *adj.* visible. *The visual beauty of the painting was remarkable.* —**vi•su•al•ly** *adv.*

viv•id /vĭv′ ĭd/ *adj.* **viv•id•er, viv•id•est.** bright and distinct; brilliant. *The vivid colors of the summer roses drew our eyes to the garden.* —**viv•id•ly** *adv.* —**viv•id•ness** *n.*